A WALK
INTO THE CITY

A WALK INTO THE CITY

Discovering the Principles
of the New Relationships
between
Urban and Suburban
Churches

Dr. Mark Brewer

Introduction by Lloyd Lewan
Foreword by Dan Issel
National Basketball Association Hall of Famer

A Walk into the City
Copyright © 2000 by Dr. Mark Brewer

Coordinated by Remington Press, Post Office Box 24187, Denver, Colorado 80222
Cover design by Jonde Northcutt
Edited by Sharyn Markus and Kathy Passerine

Scripture taken from the HOLY BIBLE, NEW INTERNATIONAL VERSION. Copyright © 1973, 1978, 1984 International Bible Society. Used by permission of Zondervan Bible Publishers.

ISBN 0-9704619-0-9
Library of Congress Control Number: 00-093446

Mark Brewer knows what ails America and, more importantly, has a lot of great ideas on how to set things right.

Former United States Senator William Armstrong

Articulate. Informed. Passionate. Mark Brewer is the right person to address the underlying ills of American society and to point to possible solutions.

Pollster George H. Gallup, Jr.

What really grabbed my attention about Mark is that he comes to where the blacks are to listen and to hear what they have to say. He works with us. He doesn't tell us who our leaders should be.

Clarence Shuler
Head of Black Family Ministries, Focus on the Family

Mark certainly loves the Lord. He is an unusually gifted preacher and a man of vision and outstanding leadership. Lives are blessed through his ministry.

Dr. Bart Hess
Pastor Emeritus, Ward Presbyterian Church, Detroit

He is a real role model, not just for our city but for others around the country.

Jim Groen
President and Executive Director, Global Connection International

People respond to his warmth like a magnet. They are warmly attentive to what he has to say.

Jack Dennison
President, Citireach

Mark is the most effective Anglo pastor in the inner city, not just in Denver but in the nation today.

Dr. Acen Phillips
Vice President, National Baptist Convention

WORDS OF THANKS

To my band of fellow adventurers at Colorado Community Church who are willing to journey with me.

To the Denver Ministerial Alliance for accepting this suburban pastor and for building enduring friendships.

To my wonderful wife, Carolyn, who is truly my loving, fellow pilgrim in life.

To Kathy for bringing "order out of chaos" with the manuscript.

To John, Don, and Jason who "walk the walk" for Christ.

To Lloyd for making this entire project a part of friendship.

INTRODUCTION

I am honored to write this introduction to *A Walk into the City*, for it strikes at the heart of one of the most important, but least understood, issues in our country – the large urban centers.

In a sense, how go America's cities goes America. It is clear that a culture that can address the challenges of a major urban center really understands the tough realities of life in a city – public education, crime, infrastructure (roads, parks), police, budget, etc. Of course, complicated disparity in economic status greatly fuels these issues.

In a way, America's cities represent the third world creeping into America. America has traditionally been a middle-class society; and, as this begins to change, one finds a new battle in the urban cities. It is not about race. It is about a growing underclass of those with fewer economic opportunities. The result of this growing underclass will be increased alienation on many levels.

At the heart of leadership, and Christianity alike, is the attitude of service and reconciliation. Many twenty-first century churches are beginning to think about these issues. Colorado Community Church, under the leadership of Dr. Mark Brewer, is committed to it.

One of this church's primary missions is to attempt to reconcile the urban and the suburban churches as one way of staying off or reducing the alienation that is inevitable across this growing underclass. Interestingly, the church is one institution that has not been as active as it should be, and so this writer applauds the efforts of Dr. Brewer and the Colorado Community Church.

This simple work, *A Walk into the City*, is recommended without reservation and with enthusiasm.

Dr. Lloyd S. Lewan

FOREWORD

I was an eighteen-year-old kid from Batavia, Illinois, playing basketball for the University of Kentucky. On a road game to the University of Mississippi, I happened across something I only had heard of before. As I strolled down a corridor to get a drink of water that day early in 1967, I saw not one, but two drinking fountains. One was marked "white." The other was marked "colored." That was my first real experience with racism.

I had grown up with people of diverse backgrounds in Batavia, which was pretty far north. The high school I attended was integrated; and on the varsity basketball team, some of my teammates were African-Americans and Latinos. At least there were not any outward signs of segregation.

In college, however, I began to see it firsthand. I remember a coach who tried to fire up his players by using the fact that they were playing an "all white team." That was how he motivated his squad. Sad!

Thankfully, the University of Kentucky reviewed its policy; and in 1970, the first black player came on board. Since freshmen were not allowed on the varsity team, I can honestly say that during my entire college career I never played with a teammate of color.

But, it was a different story in the National Basketball Association (NBA). My feelings of people being people, regardless of their skin color, were affirmed by being in an environment where the best players, not the best white players, were selected.

I have been associated with the NBA and, specifically, with the Denver Nuggets as a player, a commentator, a coach, and now coach/general manager for nearly thirty years. The great thing about the NBA is that it brings people together from diverse backgrounds and various cultural orientations to work together toward the same goal. Coaches, trainers, and administrators are all focused on building a team and fostering relationships that will result in a winning organization. Earning a position in the organization is based on individual talent and character, not on color; and that is the way it should be.

This is what has attracted me to Mark Brewer's ministry. God loves us all the same. It does not make sense in America that such separation between the urban and the suburban churches and such distrust among individuals of different ethnicities continue to exist.

In 1989, my family and I were looking for a church that would be a good fit for us. One Sunday morning, my wife, Cheri, and I decided to attend Cherry Creek Presbyterian Church. Raised Lutheran, I had never been in an Evangelical Presbyterian Church. As we arrived late, we had to ride the shuttle bus from a nearby elementary school. The sanctuary was packed. The only place to sit was on folding chairs placed in the very back against the wall. But, two minutes into Mark's sermon, I knew I had found the church home for which I was yearning.

Mark has a unique way of delivering a message. He does it with humor, feeling, and compassion. I knew I wanted and needed to hear more of that.

In late 1991, Mark accepted a call from Ward Presbyterian Church in Detroit. Eventually, he returned to Denver. Yet, the time in Detroit was well spent for my friend, Mark. The Lord developed within him a true passion for addressing the racial hatred and the youth violence that still exists in America today.

We have become a society that places too much emphasis on self. Wait at a stoplight and watch how many people drive through the light after the light turns red. This is where we place ourselves in regards to others; and if we do not change soon, this will be a troubled world in which to live.

I feel very honored that Mark has asked me to write the foreword for his book, *A Walk into the City*. He is one of the brightest guys I know. We are friends who help each other keep our feet on the ground and our focus on the things of God.

This book is worth reading. It is insightful and practical, particularly if you have any interest in joining our mutual commitment to the reconciliation of urban and suburban churches as one important way to address some of our social issues, especially racial discord.

Dan Issel

CONTENTS

AN URGENT MESSAGE
Before Rushing to the Wedding Altar

We live in incredible times. For those of us who are shepherds of the Lord's flock, we have ringside seats to an extraordinary event taking place. God's people are being pulled together into fresh, new friendships that were unthinkable just one generation ago. The new millennium is ushering in an unprecedented move of God's Spirit. The lines among churches, denominations, races, and economics that used to keep us far apart are blurring. God is erasing lines faster than we can draw them. It is true! Everywhere I go in this country, there is a cry for unity within the body of Christ like I have never seen or heard. Literally, hundreds of movements, strategies, organizations, and churches are boldly taking hands and forming new relationships in our cities. What a wonderful time to be alive! This is the good news.

The bad news is that many of us are in such a hurry to rush together to the altar that we are setting ourselves up for failure. Many of us are unconsciously sowing the seeds of later frustrations. Without knowing it, our very sincere efforts are actually reinforcing the stereotypes we are trying so hard to overcome. Digging the trenches deeper between us will not come from a lack of love. Rather, it will come from a lack of understanding of the basics of relational systems. Sharing a worship service, gathering in a stadium, or even fixing up an old building together will not defy the principles of all relationships. Using a handful of truths from the dynamics of family systems is the only way we will survive and, more importantly, thrive in our changing cities.

How many of us who have performed weddings have seen the most excited, in love, sincere couples rush to their dream wedding only to watch the marriage blow out a few miles down the road of life? Often, the difference between a loving, long lasting, healthy relationship or a short-lived, painful disaster can be some simple premarital preparation. Every engaged couple must understand before the wedding the basic principles of living together.

This is no less true if we are to bring the urban and the suburban churches together. Knowing and applying the basic principles of relationships will help us avoid a multitude of sins. The trouble is that most of the church partnerships developing today come with a number of unconscious assumptions, and I am afraid that many of us will end up like the nervous bride in a story I heard recently.

With all those people staring at her, the young bride simply could not walk down the aisle. The wedding hostess told her, "Honey, you'll do just fine. When you hear the music start, walk down the aisle, look at the altar, then look at him. It will be easy." The young bride, in nervous fear, kept saying to herself, "Look at the aisle, look at the altar, look at him. The aisle, then the altar, then him." She succeeded in making it down the aisle. But, when she heard the pastor start to ask, "Will you take this man..." she blurted out, "I'll alter him!"

As many well-meaning people are rushing to the altar to join hands to reach our cities for Christ, likewise, this unspoken assumption is rumbling underneath. What we are thinking subtly is, "We will come together in Christ. I will alter them to be like me, and then we can change the world together!" This assumption is dead wrong. It will not work between a husband and a wife, and it certainly will not work between two churches of different cultures.

I have experienced the thrill of really living life together as a suburban and an urban church family, and I have experienced the heartache and the frustration of broken dreams. I have discovered that the secret to fulfilling the dream is in knowing and in applying the natural principles of relationships.

A Tremendously Hopeful Word

This book shares the experiences and the insights I have gained over the last ten years from one of the wildest journeys I have ever taken. The journey was only a few miles away, but it might as well have been on the other side of the world. I took a walk into the city. I did not just walk on the streets, through the parks, and along the broken sidewalks of urban America. I intentionally walked into the lives of people. As a white, suburban pastor, I strapped on my faith one day ten years ago and answered a strange hunger to explore what was keeping the suburban and the downtown body of Christ apart.

Wow! What a wild ride. It has been an extraordinary journey of knowledge, laughter, anger, tears, memories, and friendships that will last a lifetime. I pray with all my heart that the few, precious nuggets of truth that I have learned so far will help others who want to make honest friendships with other cultures. I hope I can help others get a jump on the future and avoid many of the mistakes I made.

As cultures collide in the new metroplexes of America, all I can say is, "Buckle up your seat belts, everyone. The next decade is going to be like Mr. Toad's wild ride!" I am convinced that experiencing the thrills and the hurts that come with living in another culture are going to be the norm for *all* of us. Each of us, even those living in rural America, will one day take a walk into the city. I praise the Lord for the awesome blessing that is ours as we make friends with those from a culture different from our own.

Be warned. This journey is not for the fainthearted. I have had my heart broken many times. I have on more than one occasion prayed with tears, "Lord, give me a thick skin and a soft heart," because the opposite was happening. I was growing sick and tired of the racial jabs and the money lectures that my heart was starting to embitter. Since I was unprepared and did not understand what was really going on, I was becoming a closet bigot. The harder I tried, the further I sank into the quicksand of cynicism. I yearned for lasting change; yet all the prayer, time, money, and energy I had spent were being swallowed up in a pit of hopelessness.

Once, a very prominent black pastor approached me in a room full of other pastors. Putting his hand on my shoulder, he said, "Mark, don't take it personally, but you're white. Just go away." Another time, I received a death threat from a white supremacist group that read, "God has mandated the separating of the whites from the mongrel nations. All those who go against His laws must be removed."

I have seen the anger and the venom of younger African-American leaders who were devoted followers of the Nation of Islam and Farrakhan. While having a Bible study with a few black pastors, young and old, a dozen young Muslims surrounded us in the park. "You stinking Willy Lynch!" they shouted. "Go back to where you belong, and take your slave religion with you!" (Willy Lynch was a slave owner who in the 1830's wrote a paper on keeping the slaves down by separating the field slaves from the house slaves – the classic divide and conquer.)

Innumerable times, while driving home after hours of angry, dead-end meetings, I have cried, "Lord, it's just not worth it. I would rather divide land in Palestine between Arabs and Jews than try to bring the church in the suburbs and the city together. A plague on all their houses!"

So, what keeps me going? I am hopelessly addicted. Like others, I have tasted God's power. When I think I am standing all alone, I am embraced by the strong arms of my black brothers and sisters. I have seen Latino, Asian, and Anglo men and women, who a few years ago would not have even wasted water to spit on each other, pray together, share meals in their homes, and offer great acts of courage and kindness for God. I have seen the greatest force on earth unleashed, for I have seen the power of Christ's life-changing love.

I recall one quiet moment that illustrates well this power. In 1995, a network of about fifty churches and ministries had just brought together more than ten thousand people from across Denver to the arena. It was a night of incredible music, prayer, and hope. Baptists, Pentecostals, Presbyterians, Methodists, Catholics, Lutherans, Messianic Jews, and a dozen other church denominations were present. That was great, but that was not what moved me.

As people were leaving the arena, a well-known African-American pastor marched towards me. Laughing and crying nervously, he put his arms around me and hugged me for a long time. "You know, you're the first white man I have ever hugged," he said. "You will never know what this night has meant to me," he continued; and then he walked away.

He was wrong. I did know what it had meant to him. It meant what it means to all of us who have been healed and released from the wounds of the past. It means hope. It means that God can do something different.

Spirit-Filled Relationships, Not Just Spirit-Filled People

I tell everyone who will listen that I have discovered the greatest learning resource on earth to heal a city. That resource is our family. The greatest internship for doing cross-racial and cross-cultural work within the church is actually in our homes. A better teacher, yet, is the family (good or bad) in which we each grew up. Now, here is the great kick. If we can learn to say with a smile of understanding, "Oh, yeah, now I get it," to the dynamics of our own families; believe it or not, we will understand cross-cultural dynamics. When we understand the forces and the dynamics of our own families, we can say, "of course," to the same types of forces and currents that will bring churches together across ethnic lines (without being beat up in the process).

The Lord yearns to inhabit not only our individual lives but also to dwell in our relationships with one another. Without a healthy, living system of arteries and blood, a healthy lung and a healthy heart are of no use to each other. In the same way that arteries and blood fill the spaces between our physical lung and heart, God wants to fill the spaces in our relationships with each other.

When I focus on the neutral, impersonal principles of all relationships, rather than the quirks and the strange behaviors of individuals, I actually transform my personal life with others. By not personalizing everything, I really become more personal.

The bottom line is that the key to living together in our mushrooming megacities is found in the insights and in the dynamics of family systems. The freedom I discovered was not found in the latest Christian management manual. I did not find it in the latest spiritual warfare book. I did not even find it in reading African-American and Hispanic biographies and theology books. I found it as I learned and applied the dynamics of relationships in every-day families. I learned it from studying family-systems theory and by applying it to the city as a whole. I cannot overemphasize how this has transformed my life. Learning about and applying five simple principles of family systems has worked in every arena of my life. It has not only freed me up, personally, from some very suffocating, painful, and unhealthy relationships within my own family, but also it has empowered me to build relationships across a whole city. A grasp of family systems is powerful!

Get ready. The walk I have taken is the journey that everyone living in the cities of America will soon take, as well. Whether or not we like it, the world is coming to America. All of us are having Ellis Island experiences. We are feeling more and more that the country where we grew up is far away and long gone. This is especially true for the church. The great news is that God is once again doing a new and marvelous work. Whether we choose to join God is up to us. The fact that all of us must learn to work with new cultures and new relationships is a given. How we respond is our choice. We can either retreat into our spiritual enclaves and live lives of fear and frustration, or we can choose to understand what is going on and use it as a blessing in our lives and the lives of our loved ones. I would not want to live in another time period!

About This Book – A Simple Overview

It may be the best counsel and advice that I have been given in a long time. "Mark, whatever you do, write what you want to say, not what some publisher or anybody else wants to hear. It is your book. It is your life. Just say it!"

Since Lloyd Lewan is an author and has helped others in the publishing process, I took this wonderful, liberating advice. The result is in your hands. I trust and pray that this book will help you discover the treasures of God's family that are in your city as you walk into it. Even more, I pray that the freedom and the joy that I have experienced in understanding relationship systems will make you a little freer.

In this book, I wove together the five basic truths of family-systems theory with my own personal experiences. Since the

Word of God is the final analysis on relationships, I have also woven in those Scriptures that have led me the most in my walk into the city.

Part One focuses on this foundational truth: "You cannot help a relationship you are not in, and you cannot help a relationship you are stuck in." The basic insight of learning to look at how we are placed in a relationship is explained with some examples. A biblical support for God's relationships is also shared. Additionally, this section presents a challenge to re-educate ourselves. We need to stop analyzing people and to start analyzing relationships.

Part Two looks at the five principles of relationships, with each chapter focusing on a different principle.

- The first principle, **homeostasis**, examines why people do not like change (even if they are unhappy). Despite all the talk about change, we should not be surprised by the resistant behaviors.

- The second principle explains the **identified patient**. Often, the person or group with the most problems is not really the sick one in the system. This concept has proven vital to me and has kept me from rushing to conclusions about how and where to best help.

- The third principle studies the concept of **differentiation**. Integrity implies being ourselves and learning not to run away from conflict or to roll over and give in. The secret is found by staying in touch and by defining what it is we are about. This principle is especially effective in tense situations.

- The fourth principle, called **triangling**, explains one of the great games that anxious people play with each other.

"What Peter tells you about Paul is really about you and Peter." Churches and ethnic groups are masters of this unconscious game. It is crucial to learn how not to be roped.

- The fifth principle focuses on the **unseen players** in families. Sometimes, the lectures, fears, and issues that are being thrown at us are not about us at all. They are about the speaker's extended spiritual family.

Finally, the **conclusion** provides a summary and offers a few ideas to help you connect the dots and know where to begin your own walk into the city.

PART ONE
Basic Insights about Relationships

BASIC INSIGHTS
ABOUT RELATIONSHIPS

❑ You cannot help a relationship you are not in, and you cannot help a relationship you are stuck in.

❑ Family systems, as applied to the churches in a given city, means that we behave towards each other more on the basis of how we relate in the network than on the basis of our personalities or individual agendas.

❑ Learning to see the church as really one family made up of many families helps reveal why we do not work well together.

Chapter One
Beginning the Journey

Answering Another Voice - The Inner Journey
Abraham obeyed and went, even though he did not know where he was going.
– Hebrews 11:8

I would hardly equate my journey into the city to that of Abraham's answer to God's call, but there are two elements we do share in common. Although Abraham did not know where he was going, he definitely knew what he wanted. He wanted to be where God wanted him to be. Like Abraham, I did not know where I was going; and I knew I wanted to be obedient to this strange hunger inside me. I wanted to be where God wanted me to be.

It could be argued that the two most terrifying words of Jesus Christ to anyone are, "Follow me." To truly pick up and to follow him without knowing where we will end up is frightening. When I stepped out of my local, suburban church fortress and followed him into the city, I was scared to death; and, yet, it was one of the most life-giving rushes I have ever experienced.

What do I want now, ten years later? I want to be used of Christ to help build relationships within the family of God. I want to be part of the connecting tissue within the body of Christ. I also deeply desire to share the riches of five relational truths that have changed my life forever. These truths will turbo-charge any relationship.

The First Lesson about All Relationships

You cannot help a relationship you are not in,
and you cannot help a relationship you are stuck in.

There you have it. The challenge is how to actually be in relationship with each other without becoming stuck. Many of us keep away from stressful relationships and then wonder why they never become better; or we run into relationships and become stuck, helping no one. Do you know what I mean by stuck? It is a relationship sucking the life right out of us, yet we are helpless to change it. Stuck is being frozen into a pattern of behavior that no one in the relationship likes or even wants. There simply seems to be no way out.

In the Christian classic, *Mere Christianity*, the English scholar C.S. Lewis wrote, "Satan loves to send error in pairs." Satan reasons that we will choose one extreme over the other and still remain off course. This can be very true in our relationships. If we stay too far apart, we may have freedom; but we really do not have a relationship, only an acquaintance. If we stay too close and maintain control, everyone ends up suffocating.

Every relationship needs a certain degree of stickiness, or it will fall apart. The problem with relationships among churches is that there is too little glue. No real bond exists between the black and the white congregations. When a biological family loses its relational glue, the family members drift apart until they might as well be strangers to each other. Mom and Dad may know the kids; but, together, they are not that living, breathing organism called a family. When the family of God loses its stickiness, there is simply no life among us. We might as well be on different planets.

The challenge for the church, as in our own families, is to have the proper dab of this relational glue. There needs to be a deep bond between us, without it being too rigid, controlling, or superficial because too much glue causes the relationship to become brittle and to snap apart at the first strain or stress.

I have some dear friends who on the surface appear to have a very close marriage and family. The husband and the wife spend hours together laughing, joking, and conversing. The problem is that they never disagree on a single subject. They are not married. They are welded. What keeps them together is not a deep, healthy relationship. What keeps them together is a rigid system controlling each other's life for fear that the other one will leave. They are stuck in their behavior and thoughts. The real marriage died years ago. Their kids, on the surface (just like their parents), appear to be model children who are high achievers and respectful of their parents. Look a little closer, though, and we find why after graduation they left and never came home. There is no real home to come back to. What holds the family together is adherence to conformity, not honest love for each other.

Likewise, our sincere efforts to bridge cultural gaps in the church family often end up in the same sea of emptiness. We simply do not know what the appropriate distance is. We see the need to help a fellow church that is drowning in the waves of this crazy world. We either try to help by standing on the bank yelling words of encouragement to those struggling in the icy waters, or we dive in and grab hold of the people in need so tightly that we all end up drowning.

When people dive into the water to help others who are drowning, they cannot help unless they touch the people in trouble. The rescuers must be close to those they are trying to help. But, the rescuers cannot help if they let the people in trouble panic and smother them. They will all end up drowning. The church is no different. We sometimes confuse helping each other swim with drowning together because, often, the anxiety of finally being together is so great that we end up holding each other hostage to our individual agendas.

I recall a time when a frustrated elder said he was not going to be in a relationship with any other church downtown. When I asked him why, he simply replied, "I cannot continue spending my money and my time on all the building projects they need!" I then asked him if he had ever told his urban counterparts that he could no longer help them financially but that he would love to share life with them in some other way. Afraid that saying something like that would offend them, he chose to say nothing. I encouraged him to give it a try. To his astonishment, the urban church members he was seeking to help not only graciously said thank you but also were relieved because they thought he cared more about the building projects than he cared about them.

The stickiness gets even more intense when the forbidden subject of politics is allowed to surface. (For a more thorough understanding of this subject, see the section in the conclusion entitled "A Word about Politics.") How many times have African-Americans who moved to the suburbs (or worse, who stay in the hood but vote Republican) been called sellouts to the man? How many times have whites who started hanging around black congregations (or started voting Democratic) been called bleeding-heart liberals? The only way to have a semblance of relationship and to be accepted is to be quiet and to vote the party line. The trouble is that no relational bonding occurs. What results is relational bondage. Remember, we cannot help a relationship we are stuck in.

Another Lesson - The Friend of My Enemy

While pastoring in Detroit, I learned much about the Arab culture as Detroit has a marvelous community of over 200,000 Arabs from many nations. Some of the Arab friends I met taught me a rule they had learned as Muslims growing up at home. "The friend of my friend is my friend. The friend of my enemy is my enemy." I found this statement hauntingly reflective to the relationships among churches.

When I became friends with a particular pastor downtown, I was completely confused when some of my previous friends started to distance themselves from me. I did not realize this man was an old opponent of theirs. Rather than respond in the typical way and pick between the two groups, I used this Arab relational dynamic to my advantage. By staying friends with both of them and by not being pulled into past issues, I modeled for them a liberated relationship and actually made my own relationship with each of them that much freer.

You cannot help a relationship you are not in. Neither can you help a relationship you are stuck in. The challenge is to realize that massive forces are trying either to keep us apart or to keep us stuck. I have definitely felt these forces as the only white, Republican member of Denver's black, Democratic ministerial alliance. This group of pastors has been the key voice for the African-American community in Denver for more than forty-five years (long before the civil rights era).

As life would have it, I remember being at the regular meeting of the ministerial alliance the day of the O.J. Simpson verdict. (Sometimes, I wonder how in the world I end up in these places.) I will never forget that Tuesday. As soon as the acquittal verdict came back for O.J., the place went crazy. The room was filled with celebrating, hugging, shouts of joy, and honest tears of praise. I was stunned. I thought Judge Judy could have convicted this guy! Television cameras and reporters from the major stations in the city poured into the room. A press conference had been called ahead of the announcement.

The lights went on. The president of the alliance took a microphone and announced, "We are here to celebrate the vindication of an innocent man."

As the cameras panned those of us at the head table, I ducked under the table to tie my shoes. Why? I was afraid that my very white, very Republican, very suburban church would go ballistic watching their very white pastor on the evening news defend the acquittal of O.J. Simpson! Of course, one of the reporters for our ABC affiliate saw me. (As the only Anglo, I stood out in our gatherings.) She asked me what I thought.

Now, here were the two forces at work. The force to pull us apart was sucking the very life out of the room. As many whites, I thought I had just witnessed a huge injustice. One side of me wanted to cry out, "I don't relate to you people at all. We have nothing in common." The bond between us for that moment was being torn apart. But, an opposing force was also working in the room. It was the pressure to conform. To stand before my fellow black brothers and sisters and to tell them that I was dumbfounded at the verdict would be one thing. To tell the entire region by way of all the major television stations was something else. Whose friend was I? Whose team was I going to be on? Was I the friend of their friend or the friend of their enemy?

I prayed for the right words and made my reply. "Some of us feel that an innocent man has been vindicated as Pastor Phillips has just said. Some of us feel that justice was not served. The real trial, though, for us today is not about O.J. The real trial is whether our communities are going to stand together through this."

When I finished, I was confident that God had answered my prayer. How did I know? The reporter rolled her eyes and tried every trick in her journalistic bag to challenge me to stir up the issue. She finally shook her head and jetted out of the room. I had not taken the bait. I had refused to conform, and I had refused to walk away.

This is not about being clever with a comeback. This is not about maneuvering others to a non-threatening place. In fact, trying to control others is the exact opposite of this foundational truth. It is simply about discovering what you already know but may not yet recognize.

Taking Hold of the Basic Principles

There are a few, basic principles in all family relationships. Remarkably, I believe these principles are the identical dynamics that govern churches in a given city. As we understand these currents in the relational waters, we can sail through the most ferocious storms. It is true that all the water in the seven seas cannot sink a single rowboat if the water never gets inside. The weakest of us can stand up to fierce, interpersonal storms if we simply learn a few truths. But, if we do not understand these forces and currents, it will not matter how sincere, how dedicated, or how earnest we are in building our boats. Without an understanding of these basic principles, our boats will sink.

Understanding and applying these truths involves more than helping to reach our cities for Christ. We must safeguard the deepest dreams God has given us because the boats that we have built, whether they are organizations, networks, or relationships, really do carry our deepest dreams.

The great news is that we do not need to hire an expert because there are no experts in this field. There are only experienced pilgrims who know how to sail and to grasp the dynamics between people. Some of the greatest builders of relationships that I know do not have a high-school diploma. Conversely, some of the most relationally awkward people I know have PhD's. The Bible is loaded with truths about relational freedom. We just need to study it. God is not looking for experts. He is looking for fellow pilgrims and adventurers to follow him. Remember, an amateur built the ark. Experts built the Titanic.

Is This Really Biblical?

Mark Twain said that when he was between the ages of sixteen and twenty-one he could not believe how smart his father became. I feel this about my Heavenly Father. The longer I walk with him and study his Word, the more brilliant the Bible becomes every year. Honest men and women of learning are constantly reinforcing how stunningly insightful, accurate, and unexplainably brilliant the Bible is for all of life. (Are they beginning to acknowledge that God wrote it?) The last ten years of cross-racial work reinforced this to me in a fresh and deep way.

I earned my undergraduate degree in the social sciences, both psychology and sociology. In preparation for the ministry, I completed my master's work in divinity and pastoral studies. It was not until my doctoral work that I came across the unbelievable truths and the freedom in the study of a fairly new area of the social sciences called family systems. (It is too bad that this study came after fifteen years of hair pulling frustrations in ministry.)

What exactly is family-systems theory? In the 1950's, scholars, social scientists, clergy, and helping professionals started focusing on the relationships themselves that people were in rather than obsessing about childhood memories and mysterious personality secrets. *They discovered that individuals in a family behave more on the basis of how they relate to each other than on the basis of their individual personalities.* These secular, social scientists were rediscovering the truths and the sacredness of the power of relationships.

Understanding this theory is crucial if we want to bring together the new wave of churches in a given city. Our personal issues really do not matter when it comes to why churches rarely work with one another for an extended period of time. What truly matters is the dynamics of the relationships these churches create.

One of the best works on this study, *Generation to Generation*, was written by the late Dr. Edward Friedman. A psychiatrist and a member of the clergy in the Washington D.C. area, he learned that the common dynamic to all of mankind, regardless of beliefs and backgrounds, is the experience of family. (He expanded on the insights and the work of people, such as the late Dr. Murray Bowmen of Georgetown Medical School, one of the founding fathers of family therapy.) Dr. Friedman came to understand the dynamics and the forces in the local congregation as being identical to the dynamics and the forces in the families we are born into (families of origin) and the families we marry into. The local church is not a business. It is really a family. Dr. Friedman's landmark book showed pastors how to keep the dimensions of their church families, personal families, and extended families from strangling each other.

I took an educated leap of faith and applied these revolutionary truths of family systems to the church in the city as a whole. What I experienced was nothing short of the miraculous. God showed me time and time again that it was possible to bring the most volatile, hostile, and entrenched situations to a level of healing and health. This was no magic wand. It was not becoming some modern Moses saying a prayer, holding up my arms, and parting the Red Sea of division between the races. Instead, it meant doing what Jesus did. Jesus brought healing to the first church in Jerusalem despite all of their racial and economic walls, and he healed them to wholeness.

These truths can start a chain reaction that will spread freedom throughout every dimension of our lives. Not only will relationships between churches be strengthened, but also our personal family lives will be strengthened.

God's Passion for Uniting Healthy Relationships

During one terrible night in the life of our Lord Jesus, he knelt down in one of his favorite spots on earth. He had been there often. Since the time he was a little boy, three times a year he made the long trip from Galilee to Jerusalem for the great feasts. Think of his memories of this place. He loved the cool breezes and the fragrances of the flowers and olive trees. This was a place where he hid away from the hatred of his enemies and the draining fatigue of the needy crowds.

But, on this one night, there was no comfort in Gethsemane. He knew his Father was handing him the cup of his destiny. This thirty-three-year-old carpenter and common craftsman was beginning to feel the roar of hell's fury in his spirit. Jesus' heart was being torn apart. His mind was exploding into a torrential river of images and nightmares that were merely hours away. The horrors of being crucified and of becoming the sacrifice of eternity wrenched literal blood from his pores.

He who had never known sin in his person was about to take the sins of the whole world in his body. He accepted the agony of the cup his Father had given him to drink. Now, in the final moments before his passion, he prayed and poured out his heart's last desire to his Father.

What was the deepest longing of Jesus' heart before his crucifixion? "Father, I ask that they may be one, even as we are one" (John 17:21). Of all the requests that Christ Jesus could have made at that moment, his heart's desire was that his followers would be one. Astounding! Yet, it was not just the prayer that was so astounding. It was when he prayed this prayer. When people about to face death (especially the death Jesus was about to experience) make a request, we had better believe they are not playing around. Next to Christ's great commission, "Go and make disciples of all nations" (Matthew 28:19), this request for unity in his church is the clearest marching order for his followers.

Jesus Christ prayed that we would be one so that the world would know that the Father had sent him (John 17:23). Did you grasp that? Christ said that the world had the right to judge whether he was who he claimed to be on the basis of how unified our hearts and our lives are. Astonishing! Let us be honest. How are we doing?

I confess that building unity among churches was way down my list. Bringing others to Christ? Yes! Helping feed the hungry and caring for the broken? Of course! Worshiping God, building strong families, and teaching our blessed children of God's love? I am there! But, helping build relationships among members of different churches and, particularly, among different theologies, races, and ethnic groups? I was not called to that. That was for someone who did not have the pressure of leading a large church. Why would I do that?

Three reasons came to mind. First, the Bible clearly shows that relationship is one of the deep longings of our Savior. Additionally, if we choose not to build these relationships, we will miss one of the great treasures and the deep blessings of the whole Christian life. But, most importantly, breaking down these relational walls is the only hope for our world. A cynical world does not care what we say. They have heard it all. Let us be honest. Considering all the conversions to Christ, considering all the slick ministry brochures, considering all the rallies and programs, is our culture more godly now than it was twenty years ago before the great church growth movement? The world can ignore how loudly we speak, but it cannot deny what we do. When we authentically come together in honest relationship, the results are stunning.

The Age of Rage - Why This Message is so Vital

This is a wonderful time to be alive. Never before has America experienced such a time of invention, prosperity, and peace. But, this is also a very dangerous time. In the midst of the good, cultural pressure plates under the earth are pushing against each other. Even within the church, underneath all the Christian politeness, tremors are rumbling. Once in a while, people can feel the tremors; but everyone pretends they are not serious. I am concerned that the big one, a major racial earthquake, is waiting to explode. Anger abounds (and I do not mean just frustrated drivers). White suburban anger and inner-city frustration abound. I sense a growing rage in both worlds, the urban and the suburban. At times, I smell gasoline in the streets, and I fear someone is going to throw a lit match. The church is too ill-prepared to handle it, even though we do not need to be.

Not long ago, I was talking with a brother about strategies to reach the inner city. His huge, burley frame barely fit in the wingback chair in my office. Joe has a passion for Jesus and the young lives downtown. I asked him what he thought about the suburban church.

"Bro," he answered, "I'll tell you what bugs me about suburban Christians. They throw you some chump change and act like they're doing something for you. White people had better wake up. People downtown aren't stupid! They know when they're being used so others can feel good about themselves."

Joe was raised in the heart of Los Angeles in a tightly knit, Asian family. Born in Samoa, he was raised to be a leader. In fact, his father was the village chief, and Joe was in line to be the next chief. Living in the heart of a tough part of Los Angeles was no problem for him. The African-American gangs, as well as the Hispanic gangs, were no threat to the Samoan gangs. They lived by the same street code and had ice in their veins in order to survive a life of violence. Twisted loyalties and minute-by-minute ethics led Joe to the California prison. Before his final hearing, he was still playing football on a scholarship.

"You know, Mark, no one ever wondered if you would do time," he continued. "The question was when. Besides, once you were sent away, you could work out and get three hots and a cot (room and board). And, there were already brothers inside to help you keep it goin'. No fear, man!

"But then, a white brother, of all people, told me about Jesus. Man, at first I thought this little white guy was nuts! Every day he would come to my apartment while I was waiting for the hearing and invite me to this Bible study. I thought to myself, 'I'm gonna kill this guy! If he comes by again, I'm gonna send this guy home to meet this Jesus personally!'"

Joe found that Christ could use a person of another race, even a race he had hated all his life, to heal his own heart. One night, he finally gave his life to Christ. He took God up on a proposition. "Lord, either do something big or quit buggin' me!" he had told God. The next day, for no apparent reason, all the charges against him were dropped. Later, he learned that the charges were dropped the very hour he had prayed to ask Christ into his life! Joe is once again living his life on the streets. This time he is reaching kids for Jesus.

But, there is another point to this beautiful story. The more Joe works with the suburban churches to help reach the inner city, the more it reinforces all the stereotypes he has of white, middle-class Christians. (This used to really bug me each time

I heard it. I used to think, what did we ever do to harm them? Do they honestly believe our lives are paradise in the suburbs?) Joe's frustration in building lasting relationships between the urban and the suburban churches was my frustration, as well. It was easier to reason that God just wanted us to take care of the flocks we had or to conclude that trying to be friends was too much of a hassle. Why waste the energy on something that was nothing more than an ideal?

God's Opinion about the Matter

Is there biblical support for relationship building across racial and residential walls? Of course! Like so many before, is this just a current fad or ministry wave that will crest and disperse in time? Absolutely not! These primary relationships, just like family, have always been God's plan. The power of healthy, Spirit-filled relationships has always been God's healing agent. Heaven will be inhabited by people from "every tribe, nation, people and language" (Revelation 7:9). From the very beginning, the very image of God was endowed into a relationship between a man and a woman in the garden (Genesis 1:27).

God is the God of relationships. God brought the twelve tribes of Israel together three times a year (Deuteronomy 16:16). It was not for worship alone. Life from God himself flowed into the nation as these tribes gathered together. The Apostle Paul wrote, "in Christ we who are many form one body, and each member belongs to all the others (Romans 12:5). In his letter to the church at Corinth, Paul explained, "the body is not made up of one part but of many. If the foot should say, 'Because I am not a hand, I do not belong to the body,' it would not for that reason cease to be part of the body" (I Corinthians 12:14,15).

Belonging to each other is true about the local congregation, but it is even truer about the churches in a given city. We are incomplete without each other! When the Resurrected Christ addressed the seven churches in Revelation, notice that he addressed each city as though the churches in each of these cities were one church. A large, metropolitan city like Ephesus had churches scattered throughout the city; yet Christ treated these churches as one, "To the church in Ephesus" (Revelation 2:1). The same was true for the churches in each of the other six cities mentioned.

- Do you want to know how to keep your cool in the most heated confrontations?
- Do you want to gain a fresh, new understanding of your part in God's plan?
- Do you want not only to survive the coming waves but also to thrive in them?
- Do you want to know how to take the sickest family systems in the city, church, and home and bring peace and healing to them?

Then, read on! There are real answers. This is a journey we all can experience.

Summary

1. In light of all the excitement of churches and ministries rushing to help each other, sometimes, we actually dig the trenches deeper among us. If we do not understand the dynamics of family relationships, we may end up reinforcing stereotypes about each other.

2. Two great truths about all relationships exist. First, **you cannot help a relationship you are not in**. People who think time will change a relationship amaze me. Time is not the catalyst. People change relationships. You have to be there to help it. Second, **you cannot help a relationship you are stuck in**. Acting, thinking, and behaving in a manner that is comfortable for you or in a manner that you think the other

person wants will not help the relationship. It is entrenching. Do not conform, and do not walk away.

3. The **dynamics of family relationships are identical to those among churches in a given city.** We need to recognize that people very often act the way they do because of how they are **positioned in a system** rather than because of some personal baggage they carry.

4. God wants us to enjoy Spirit-filled relationships. Throughout the Bible, he has desired this. The Bible never addresses us as individual units alone on some planet. Our **Lord Jesus' deepest longing is that we alter this world by altering the way we relate to each other.**

Chapter Two
Quit Analyzing Individual People
– Start Analyzing Relationships

The Journey's First Storms

For the past few years, I have been involved with the pastoral prayer summits, one of the great movements of God's hand in this country. Several hundred pastors from every color, theology, and church size gather together to seek God. Some of these rich times of prayer, worship, and listening to the Father are for several days. Some are only overnight.

At first, everyone is nervous. Pastors can be a terribly insecure lot. Some pastors spread their peacock feathers and speak in their sanctified, stained-glass, Christianized, church voices. This goes on for the first hour or so. Then, the atmosphere changes. We either tire, or the Holy Spirit grabs us. I do not know which. But, wow, what sweet openness happens! Nothing brings intimacy and trust like being with another human in extended prayer before the Throne.

These prayer summits also open the gates to share honest thoughts about how the different ethnic churches are working together in the same city. Here are some actual comments from influential pastors and clergy.

I'm sick of all this race talk. When are we ever going to get on with life?

It's not about my ancestors being in chains. It's about me, my wife, and my kids not being accepted for who we are. The pain is right here, right now!

All this racial and money talk is just the flesh. If we knew each other after the spirit, it would all just go away.

I'm so tired of being used by the inner-city churches. All they want is our money. For all the talk about reconciliation, I'll tell you what they're reconciling – their bank account! What they really mean is, "Bring that white cow over here and milk it." Then, watch them fight each other over who gets to milk the cow first!

I feel sorry for what they did to the blacks. The African-Americans were brought over here in chains. But, I want to tell you something as an Hispanic. They may have come over in chains, but our land was taken. This was Mexico! How come the blacks get all the press and attention?

I don't get it. I come over to this country speaking an entirely different language. You try and learn English after being raised on Chinese. The whole issue about teaching Spanish in our schools...I'm proud to be an American. That means our language is English!

The Asians come over here and take our inner-city businesses. They buy out the local store, move out to the suburbs, and then take our money with them. You ask how come they don't stay poor long? It's inner-city money!

Don't tell me you care for me as a Christian and then beat my brains out in the voting booth. How does a Christian take the food out of our babies' mouths and the books from our children's hands and the heat from our elderly who are dying and then say that we "should love one another"? For all the white, suburban Christian's passion for the unborn and pornography, it seems that the "already born and struggling" don't matter.

How on earth can someone be a follower of Jesus and vote like that? If they would talk about people coming to Christ half as much as they talk about affirmative action, there would be real change in this society.

It is rather depressing, isn't it? How on earth could one Anglo pastor from the suburb take on issues like these?

Anxiously, I thought about what I should do. Should we do a massive fund drive and help the needs? No, even the government does not have enough money to do that. Should we just sit down and come up with a strategic game plan to answer all the issues together? No, because whose sincere, burning issue do we take on first and for how long?

Instead, after bathing the whole challenge in prayer, I started applying the principles of families to these honest problems; and something weird happened. We did not answer the questions of economics or racism. We started, instead, to answer the question as to why we were so far apart from each other.

Believe it or not, all these racial and economic challenges are drenched in hope; but we have to start looking at the lay of the land entirely differently. We need to re-educate ourselves completely.

We need to have ears that listen to relationship questions, not merely to the surface dialogue. Do not misunderstand me. The issues are extremely important for the church. But, there is something even more important at work: how we relate to each other. What we really need is to see the deeper issues that God sees.

Getting Our Eyes off Our Feet and onto the Road

To begin, there are a few principles we need to understand. Learning to look at our lives in this new way is the very foundation to creating healthy, liberating, and God-honoring relationships. In fact, it is the only way that Anglo, African-American, Hispanic, and Asian churches can effectively take hands and together change a city.

Our minds need to be re-oriented. Since we have been drenched in the false, media world presentation of half-hour problems and solutions, we tend to see life in terms of simple action and reaction. For example, the African-American pastors said that, so we did this. The suburban church leaders do this all the time, so we will do that. If government would only do this, then that would happen. We try to explain our reactions with a one-dimensional reason. *(Note the illustration.)*

The trouble is that we are not a bunch of billiard balls acting the way we do because another ball bounced into us. We are more like our earth as the sun, the moon, and the other planets in our solar system pull it at the same time. No counselor or pastor would be so naïve as to think that a mother-daughter problem does not involve the whole family. A mother and a child behave differently when Dad is not around, and they behave differently if Dad is around and the other siblings are out of the picture.

We have grown accustomed to thinking that all there is to know about sailing is keeping the boat from running into another

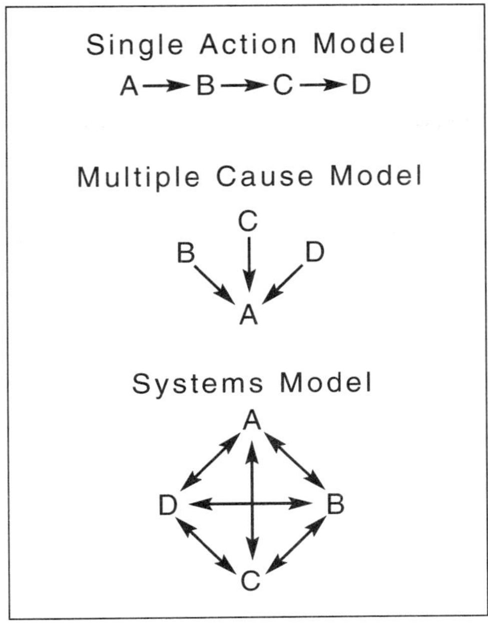

boat. If two boats collide, the simplest view is that one of the captains was at fault. Most of the time, however, other factors, such as the unseen wind or the ocean currents, are involved. Life is not as simple as we are led to believe.

If we really want to understand why race is still a huge divider in the church or why only ten per cent of the churches in America *ever* work with another denomination or ethnic church, we have to look at how one issue relates to all of the other issues. *(Again, note the illustration.)* There are deeper laws at work.

A revolution in viewing life has happened in our generation. It began with the sciences. Science realized that the complexities God created in the biological world were governed by rules greater than the individual organism. More was going on in the pond than simply adding up all the frogs, fish, and insects. Life among the organisms had its own rules; an ecosystem is what scientists call it. Life is more than the individual parts. If a frog is taken out of its pond and placed into a laboratory tank, it will act differently. If a healthy frog from one pond is placed into an identical pond, the frog may become sick.

Here is one of the great ironies of systems. The more complicated a system seems to be to unravel, the standard solution is to make a few basic changes. But, in reality, the more complicated a given system is, the more necessary it is to look at the principles of relating. What are the dynamics of the relationships in the given setting?

Every sports fan knows that a single player's performance cannot be explained by that player alone. Great running backs make touchdowns because of the linemen. Execution happens because each individual on the team knows how to relate to every other individual on the team. This is really apparent when an athlete finds him/herself on a different team. The chemistry of one athlete will be entirely different on a different team. Many a basketball team has learned this the hard way in trades. Winning is not solely achieved by effort and desire. It is a question of relating (or not relating) on and off the court.

The body of Christ in a given city, town, or region is no different. If we are serious about wanting to change, *we need to start studying our relationships, rather than obsessing about personalities and second-guessing others' agendas.*

Dr. Friedman discovered that the best way to heal pastors, their families, and their congregations was to stop the temptation to overanalyze, categorize, or label an individual's inner problems. Instead, he coached people not to become sucked into certain dynamics. Rather than deal with all the inside issues, he coached them to deal with their relational networks. The results were astounding. Deeply entrenched, emotional illnesses and traumas (such as depression, obsessions, panic attacks, and substance abuse) were actually healed by refusing to deal with them directly and by dealing with the person's family system instead.

For example, a bride came to see a counselor before her wedding. She was anxious and could not sleep at night. Rather than prescribing sleeping pills or talking about pre-wedding jitters, the counselor probed into her family system. He learned that the bride's mother was upset about her daughter's choice for a husband. He also discovered that her fiancé's ex-wife was threatening to wreck the wedding.

What to do? With so many issues involved, he coached the new bride to be in the relationship without becoming stuck. He helped her not to become triangled into her mother's issues with her future son-in-law. He showed her how to delegate her anxiety about her fiancé's ex-wife to her husband. Above all, the counselor resisted becoming entangled with the bride-to-be's secret, emotional life. The result? Two weeks before the wedding, the bride looked radiant. She said she had not slept so well in years. Her mother was overjoyed about her new son-in-law. The ex-wife showed up and behaved perfectly.

This amazing result was not because of Dr. Friedman's education, years of training, or brilliance (although, in my opinion, he was brilliant). It was because he learned to see and to understand the relational networks within people. He found that many of our chronic problems were not a result of our childhood, our inner conflicts, or even our physiology. (I think he went a little far in discrediting these, but most purists or theorists do.) Remarkably, he discovered that our inner issues have more to do with *others'* personalities and our relational networks, where we stand within them and how we relate to them.

Remember, we cannot help a relationship we are not in anymore than we can learn to swim by e-mail. We have to be in the water with others, but we must not let them pull us under. Rather than trying to solve the situation ourselves or teaching others to control the situation, we must control our reaction to the event. Not everyone involved needs to sit down to work it through. We just need to find one person who can bring a healthier way of relating to the situation. Think of the ramifications this can have in bringing churches in the city together!

In the End You Are the Ministry

In the final analysis, all God has to heal this world is his power inside each of us. We know that. He has told us this time and time again in Scripture. As God said through Paul, "Christ in you, the hope of glory" (Colossians 1:27). How much clearer can he be? But, we never act on this fact. It is not that we do not try. In fact, that is the problem. We try to heal issues by starting with our knowledge, insights, programs, money, abilities, or expertise. We look for ways to fix the problems and the pain deep inside others, rather than making use of the power of how we relate to these issues!

Dr. Friedman discovered that helping people learn how to navigate the relationship currents themselves was far more effective than dealing with the problems on board their personal boats. In essence, he taught people how one person can change the direction of the water.

It takes a while to teach ourselves how to see life through these new lenses; but, oh, when it happens, how sweet it is! What I'm talking about is simply the power of presence, God's presence in us, and the phenomenal healing power of positioning ourselves in the right place within a broken system. It involves taking Christ's hand and engaging in the situation. The key is not to become pulled into all of the currents or to cut bait and leave. Instead, we must teach others how to relate healthily. The primary issue is to be free ourselves with those we are helping.

Then, we need to let God bring them to the place where he can heal their own style of relating.

Do you realize what this means? Blacks do not need to act like whites or to know everything about the white culture in order to bring healing. Whites do not need to know all the facts about the black culture in order to be used as a catalyst for Christ's healing. Forget about being an expert. This nation has too many cultures, histories, and styles. The great news is that we do not need to know everything about each other. We simply need to wade into the water and to keep from being pulled out to sea by all the currents and all the relationship games that are going on. Without being irreverent, once you experience the freedom this brings, it must be a faint hint of what it was for our Lord to walk on the water. It is sure a better way to travel than straining on the oars against the waves.

Summary

1. Underneath all the outward talk of reconciliation, when people are honest, anger and frustration are seething. The harder we try, the worse situations become.

2. Wrong motives and half-hearted efforts are not the cause for most of the failed efforts to reconcile black and white churches. **Failure came when we ignored the forces and the dynamics of the relational systems involved**. Sin is not confined to individuals. Sin has infected our very relationships.

3. God's marvelous creation has at its very foundation unchanging principles and dynamics of relationships. It is not merely about the individuals who make up those relationships. We need to **start studying the actual relationships themselves, rather than hyper-analyzing each other personally**. We must figure out more than why

the other sailors cannot steer their boats right. We must change the currents in the water that are slamming our boats into each other and into the rocks.

4. Sometimes, the fastest and most effective way to bring about healing is to focus on how the hurting person is relating to his/her network of relationships. We must stop fixing his/her boat. We must **teach the hurting person how to change** the way the boat interacts with the currents in the water.

5. The **best way to transform a sick system is to transform how we relate to it ourselves.** In the end, all we bring is who we are in Christ. The answer to racial healing and new ways of relating is not in helping others to understand; it is modeling a healthy way of relating to them ourselves.

PART TWO
Five Principles of Relationships

THE FIVE PRINCIPLES OF RELATIONSHIPS

HOMEOSTASIS

The first principle of relational systems is **homeostasis**. No one likes change. Once a system is established, it will resist any change that threatens to disrupt its equilibrium, even if the change is for the better. These behaviors are not conscious. It is just how systems work.

THE IDENTIFIED PATIENT

The second principle is the **identified patient**. This means that the neediest person (group, organization) or the person (group, organization) with the most symptoms may not be the sickest one. The best treatment is time spent on the most responsive person in the system, not the apparently neediest.

DIFFERENTIATION

The third principle is **differentiation**, the power of your presence. The answer and the tremendous advantage of this unconscious dynamic is that you can bring about healing without anyone knowing it. The answer is to stay in touch and to define what you are about. Do not become fused to the problem.

TRIANGLING

The fourth principle of relationships is **triangling**. When two people or two groups are uncomfortable with each other, they pull a third person, group, or issue into the system to divert the anxiety. What Peter tells you about Paul has to do with you and Peter's relationship; it is not about Paul.

THE EXTENDED FAMILY

The fifth and final principle focuses on **the extended family**. Unseen players are on the field. We all live in several relational systems at any given time. A problem in one network can manifest itself in another. Likewise, healing one network by staying in touch and by defining can actually bring positive results inside a different network.

Chapter Three
No One Likes Change but a Wet Baby
(…and a Wet Baby Cries!)

Jim was a classic white, southern gentleman. He had attended the finest schools in the South, served in the United States Air Force, and ministered as a Presbyterian pastor. He had one of those sweet spirits and refined styles. Although he was not a bigot, he admitted that he never really interacted with people of color. "Growing up, they had their life, and I had mine."

Jim also knew what it was to have the rug yanked from under him. His life took a bad turn, and he found himself divorced, unemployed, and broke. To pay his bills, he took a second night job delivering pizzas. One night, he was delivering to a rougher part of town. As he entered the stairwell to the second floor, out of the corner of his eye, he saw three black teens jump from under the stairs. One had a baseball bat. Who knows what the others had? They had phoned in a fake order just to jump him.

I barely recognized this once good-looking man, even after his facial reconstructive surgery. He could hardly speak when I visited him at the hospital. It was not because of the injuries (even though Jim barely lived through the ordeal). It was because of the hatred.

"Animals! They're just animals, Mark!" he cried. "Why would anyone do this to another human being? My mama was right. They're not like us."

I invited Jim to a gathering of pastors from various churches in the city. I felt the other pastors could bring some needed healing to his life. I had no idea how right I was.

Jim sat alone at a round table for eight. As the meeting began, five black pastors slowly sat down at his table. I asked the people around each table to introduce themselves and then to pray for each other. I was positive that Jim was going to get up and move to another table. But, something happened too quickly.

"Brother, what happened to you?" one of the African-American pastors inquired.

"I was jumped by three black demons," Jim defiantly stated; and he started to push back his chair to stand up.

What was going to happen? I was trying to moderate the room of about fifteen tables, but I could not take my eyes and ears away from this table. What happened next was unbelievable.

Without being defensive, without explaining, and without lecturing, this black pastor asked, "May we lay hands and pray for you?" Some of these men knew what it was like to roll on the ground while been kicked by the boots of another for the crime of just being black. They knew the venom of irrational hatred and rage.

Rigidly, Jim replied, "I guess so."

Then, the black pastors extended their hands to him. Jim's right hand seemed frozen to the side of his seat. Slowly, he put his hand out and took one of theirs. He then sobbed uncontrollably as they prayed, hugged, loved, and healed him. They could not remove the scars from his face; yet God used them to remove the deeper ones, the ones in his heart.

Ironically, as they sought to heal Jim, they were really healing something else: a system that had kept them from stepping across racial lines. Of the five black pastors, only one had ever before prayed with a white pastor.

An Unconscious Resistance

Keeping in mind that God's family of faith in a given city really does behave like a family, one of the first principles of family systems is **homeostasis,** a fifty-cent word that means the same state. Everything seeks a balance. Once this balance is set, the system will resist change to the death. Balance, in this sense, does not necessarily mean healthy. It simply means that a pattern or a way of relating has been established. For example, when the concrete hardens, the footprints stay. When a little creek starts running, the future river will follow the same course.

Homeostasis happens in our physical bodies. An example is body temperature. When we are hot, we sweat. When we are cold, we shiver. Why? Our bodies are regulating the balance of our internal temperature. Our bodies do not do change well.

Homeostasis happens between nations and governments. We are living in a stressed, new world. How can this be when the cold war is over? It is because the international balance is messed up. It was easier when we knew who our enemies and our allies were. Our political world does not do change well.

Homeostasis happens in our social lives. When we speak to people in America, we stand about eighteen inches from their faces. No one taught us this. We just do it. Don't believe me? Today, stand six inches from a friend's face, and watch your friend step back twelve inches; or stand about two feet from a friend's face, and watch this person step forward six inches. Similarly, two people will stop their conversation when they step on an elevator occupied by others. Their privacy zone and space have been invaded. But, when the elevator doors open, the conversation re-starts. Our social lives do not do change well.

Now, the real challenge is that none of this resistance is conscious. We do not consciously say, "Oh, the system is changing. Let's stop it." The reason that homeostasis works inside a system is exactly because it happens without thinking. Otherwise, we would constantly be focusing on balancing life, rather than moving forward with life.

What does this have to do with racial relationships among churches? We, in the church, really do not do change well. For those who want to be used by God to transform the way churches have been relating, get ready and buckle up! It is going to be one wild ride.

The moment we play with any system, whether or not the people within the system like what is already happening, the system itself will resist change ferociously. Remember, this is not about the individuals, per say. For example, in family systems, why would a woman stay with a man who beats her? The reason is that the abuser is shrewd to isolate her from outside support, which would hinder his intimidation to make her stay. (Astonishingly, abusers often even convince their victims that they deserve to be physically abused.) We do not like change, even when change is to our benefit.

We can see this in our families. Every step of the way, I resisted change in my family. First, I made the big leap from dating to marriage. That was a change. Then, I remember the shock of going from Carolyn and me to the birth of our first born. It was not merely that Vanessa changed what I had to do. This precious, little invader actually changed how I related to my wife. Forever. Do you know what? Each of our other kids, as they entered our family system, did also. Siblings are never born into the same family. While the group of individuals is the same, the way family members relate to each other has changed. The equilibrium of the family is altered.

The church in the city is identical. On the surface, a first glance would say this does not apply for the sheer reason that we do not even have relationships. Not so! The homeostasis in the American church is deep and will fight anyone who challenges it. The balance that we have basically looks like this. The suburban white church appears organized, well-financed, and moving forward. In other words, it appears strong. The urban African-American church appears unorganized, poor, and struggling. In other words, it appears weak. Because we all love Christ and want to help each other, everyone is in favor of the stronger church helping the weaker sister church. Right? Wrong. Dead wrong.

Is this because the suburban church is selfish, loves control, and does not care? Maybe, for some folks, but I do not find this to be the norm. Is it because the urban church has false pride, is lazy, and does not really want responsible help? Maybe, for some, but I do not find this to be the norm, either.

It is this kind of analysis that reinforces the homeostasis at work. At first, I went crazy trying to wrap my arms around this baffling problem. All the people I met were singing from the same sheet of music (let us help and learn from each other); but the reality was that the more they tried, the worse the relationship became.

In fact, the relationship grew worse until I started to understand this first dynamic of family systems called homeostasis. This was not some conspiracy. This was not some failure of heart or intention. Evil was once again winning the day by having us defeat ourselves. How? Evil was causing us to try to change people, the project, or the issue; and in doing so, we were actually reinforcing this unhealthy system. Remember, we were not even aware of what was happening. We just knew we did not like the result.

This is sometimes why the larger and more visible the gatherings are to be reconciled the deeper the system is entrenched and the less likely there will be any lasting change. That is the bad news.

The good news is that this unconscious response can actually be used to our advantage in creating healthy relationships. Even Jesus said that we like the old better than the new, but he brought about the Kingdom. Interestingly, he did it not by taking on the obvious evils of the day. Instead, he took on the kingdom of darkness itself. He did not merely remove the foul-smelling tumors. He attacked the spiritual cancer.

An Unused Power

When we hang Christmas lights, we have a chance to see the power of two different systems at work. One system uses a series form of wiring. It is a popular system because it is less expensive. But, it also drives the user insane. Why? Power passes along a route that simply goes from one light bulb to the next. *(See the illustration.)* The moment one bulb burns out, all the other bulbs lose their power. Then, the game to find which bulb is the culprit begins. By the way, this gives all control to any single bulb that threatens to go out on the others. It is a common hostage game that I will explain further in chapter five.

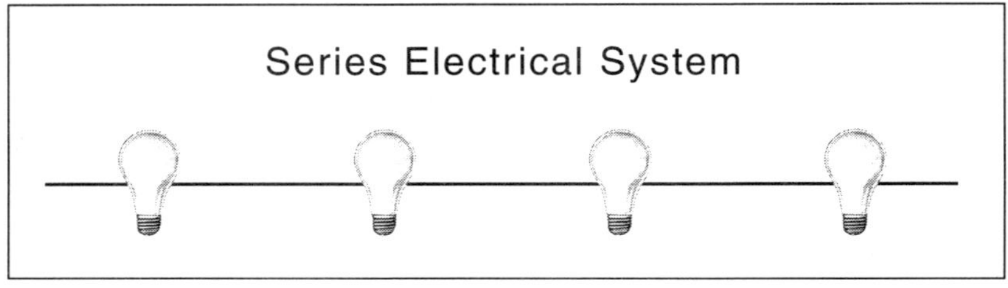

The other system of wiring is called parallel. It is more expensive because it requires double the wiring. It also causes less of a headache for the end user. Every bulb has its own power source and simply works as a ground for the other bulbs. *(See the illustration.)* The result? If one bulb burns out, the others stay lit. Better yet, every other bulb in the connection can burn out, and one little bulb can keep shining.

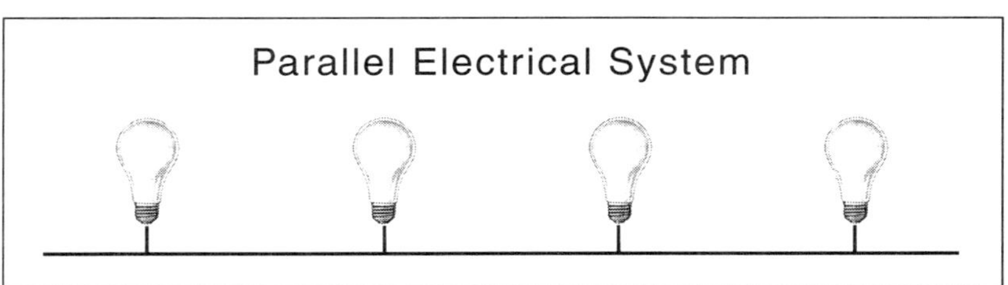

The difference in these two wiring systems is how each bulb relates to the other bulbs in the system and where each bulb receives its main source of power. Is power received through the other bulbs, or is it received directly to itself?

This is no different for God's people. One of the fascinating effects on people who have met Christ and had their lives radically transformed is that they can go back to the same dark places, but this time shine brightly. Before meeting Christ, the approval of the crowd, friends, or family was the power source. If the power was cut off, their light went out. But, when people become connected to Christ directly, even while connected to other people, they are no longer dependent on others for power.

This is just as true for the church. One of the ways to diagnosis a healthy balance among churches in a city is to consider how they are connected. Are they relationally dependent on one another, or does each church function from its own power source?

This unconscious aspect of homeostasis can be powerful for good. We can walk into new situations, connect with people by making the first contact, and, yet, not be dependent upon their approval. If this happens to be in a system that uses a series style of relating (where one influential church or group of pastors is the gatekeeper), we can be used greatly. By simply being there, without being pulled into the system, we can actually be used to create new ways of relating with others.

Dr. Larry Crabb, a Christian psychologist, related a similar story at a conference in Los Angeles. While strolling along the boardwalk in Miami Beach, he and his wife saw a rather bizarre scene. Along the porch of a large retirement village were fifty older folks sitting in rocking chairs. The Crabbs realized that no one on the porch was interacting. Everyone was staring straight ahead. How sad, the Crabb's thought. If only they would turn their chairs toward each other to enjoy the warm, afternoon sun together. Dr Crabb wondered if the Lord, as he observes our relationships, ever has a similar thought. "Why don't they turn their chairs toward each other and share this wonderful life I have given them?"

The tremendous power of the church is not in finding congenial relationships where we hang around people who are like us. The power of the church is not even found in cooperative relationships where we pool our resources into some common project or task. The unused power of the church is in connecting relationships where we actually know, share, and care for each other. It can be done. Resistance and struggle should be expected at first. Nothing is going wrong. Homeostasis is at work. We are being used to develop a new balance. Resistance and struggle are actually signs that something great is happening. Sometimes, the greatest joys are just on the other side of the hill if we do not quit. Ask any mother after delivery if it was worth it.

Like a Duck

Have you every noticed how ducks swim? On the water's surface, they glide smoothly; but underneath the water, their legs are kicking like the dickens. The way to create a new balance is to stay calm on the surface but to kick like the dickens under the water to keep from being pulled down stream. It is not about ranting and raving or giving persuasive speeches. It is about being there and staying calm in the chaos.

Jesus Christ said that we need new wineskins (Matthew 9:17) so that this new life would not burst out on the ground. Of course, he was primarily referring to the new life in him that will not work if we are trying to keep the law on our own.

God's Spirit did not come to give us an external patch-up job. Our very souls must be born again into a new nature (2 Corinthians 5:17). Many people have rightly applied this illustration to organizations, local churches, and various other groups. Sometimes, it takes birthing a whole new organization. But, I also see that it applies to a new way of relating to each other. We must create a whole new balance that frees us from the anxious control games. We must create a fresh homeostasis because the old systems of relating cannot handle this new life.

In John 2:13-22, when Christ cleansed the Temple, he totally enraged the gatekeepers of the old, sacrificial system. Although most were self-serving materialists, many were enraged because they could not imagine changing the system they had been raised in. Change is hard.

A well-known church consultant, Lyle Schaller told a fascinating story at a seminar held several years ago in Denver. The University of Wisconsin Medical School tried an experiment one year. Rather than selecting students based on grades, medical exam scores, internships, interviews, and class ranking, they randomly chose their applicants for that one year. At the end of the three-year term, the findings amazed the selection committee. The class of randomly selected students did as well emotionally, scored as well on exams, and suffered the same dropout rate as classes that had been finely selected. Are you ready for the bigger shock? The next year the school returned to the old, time-consuming, expensive selection process, even though there was no evidence that the process screened a better student. The moral of the story is this: We know how to do what we have always done much better than we know how to change. Homeostasis.

Sometimes, staying in sick relationships seems easier than changing them. That is why Jesus asked the man lame for thirty-eight years, "Do you want to get well?" (John 5:6). Sometimes, we grow a strange attachment to being sick. Homeostasis.

For all of the sincere cries for change, we must be truly ready when we start to do it. I counseled a sweet lady in our church who was outraged at her husband. The guy lay around on the couch watching television all day. He never helped around the house, and he was fifty pounds over weight. For years, she tried everything she could think of to change him. In the end, he went to church with her. He gave his life to Christ, and the rebirth started. Within months he found a job, started exercising, began helping around the house, and displayed a new zest for life. Her response? She left him a year later. You might wonder, "But, I thought she was longing for that?" She was, but she never anticipated that changing the whole family system would be so hard. She was unable to adapt to the changes.

Similarly, when an authentic relationship begins to form between different races, sometimes for no apparent reason, everyone just quits and goes home. Homeostasis. That is why a church or business sometimes puts up with the chronic complainer or irritant and fires the person who comes in with fresh ideas of change for greater effectiveness. Homeostasis.

But, remember, the positive side of homeostasis is also true. A couple in my church, who moved from the East Coast, was beside themselves. The wife's parents expected each of their children (all were married with large families) to spend every Christmas together with them in New Jersey. No one dared challenge this expectation, even though they did not like it. This couple wanted to know if not going was dishonoring her parents. I told them, no, if they did it lovingly. They were merely dishonoring the family system. They called her parents and explained that they were not going to be able to make it for Christmas that year, but they would plan on coming out the following year. As expected, they encountered threats, received phone calls from other siblings, and experienced the cold treatment. You name it, and the parents tried it. Now, five years later, they go out every other year and love it more. Each of the other four siblings and their families were also given permission to change. The parents have never been happier. It is not about changing others. It is about having the courage to change the way we relate to others.

I love to watch transformation. On prayer retreats with a rather diverse group of pastors, I like to have them see with the eyes of Christ. All the pastors put their chairs in a circle. I take several Bibles or hymn books, place them on the floor, and map out the city. Then, the pastors place their chewed-on coffee cups on the map where their church lies in the city. Now comes the fun part. I ask, "Do you realize that when Christ looks down on our city, he sees only one church meeting in these different places?"

At first, arms are crossed. They are not angry. They are simply sorting through the files in their minds to consider the truth of my statement. When the, "ah ha," takes place, without even directing, they inevitably stand over different parts of the map. They pray as a whole for the different quadrants of the city. They realize that we are all the same family. They understand that different areas of the church in each city have different challenges, attacks, and opportunities. The whole system of competition for the moment vanishes. It is stunning when it happens. A new balance of connecting starts to weave a fabric of friendship across the room and then across the city. It is all in understanding the forces of family.

Summary

1. All living relationships create a balance or a routine way of relating. This force is called **homeostasis**. This system will resist any attempt to change it. Whether the system is healthy or unhealthy is irrelevant. Expect it, and do not take it personally.

2. The **dynamics of family systems are not conscious**. The more we ask people, "Can't you see what's going on?" the less they see it. America has developed a system of strong suburban churches helping weak urban churches. This was not a plot or a strategy. The encouraging news is that it can be changed.

3. A good way to determine the level of health in a system is to **know how people are connected**. A string of lights connected by its own power source will stay lit, even when individual bulbs burn out. Often, churches in a city fall into relationships where a few churches become the power source for a group of other churches. This helps no one. It is very possible to maintain one's own identity and still help an entire system simply by being the first person to be in a relationship that is free.

Chapter Four
The Truly Sick One in the Family

A Catholic friend of mine served three years as a missionary in Africa. He said that the nuns who had given their lives in service to this one part of Nigeria had an observation about those who came over for mission trips.

"When you come for six weeks, you write a book. When you come for six months, you write an article. When you've lived here for six years, you don't write anything. You finally realize how little you know."

This summarizes well my experiences. The first year of doing cross-racial work, I was all excited to put my thoughts on paper. Now, after ten years, I am much more humbled and cautious in what I write. Although I long all the more to spread the message about how to beat this demon of division, there are no short cuts. We are going to have to walk out of this forest as far as we have walked into it. Some of us just started out a little bit earlier in our journey. God never promised us that he would send in a helicopter to air vac us out. He did, however, promise that he would take our hand and walk with us the entire way.

A few years ago, the Associated Press published an intriguing photograph of the Midwest flooding. As captured by one photographer's eye, a dog and a cat and a chicken are huddled together on the roof of an abandoned house. They are soaking wet and quietly waiting for a rescue. Moments before the flood, they would have killed each other. Now, in the midst of the raging waters, they are bed buddies.

What a picture of the church, for a flood is coming that will slam us all together in this final chapter of history. African-Americans, Hispanics, Asians, Anglos, Charismatics, Baptists, Presbyterians, and Catholics will find themselves climbing into God's shelter. This final storm will truly be the mother of all storms. Some of us will be prepared and find that it is the greatest time of God's hand in human history. Others of us will be ill-prepared and find the whole event a frustrating nightmare. Who will and will not make it? The answer lies with those who have learned the hidden secrets of family systems.

Thus far, we have seen (according to systems theory) that people in relationships behave more according to how they are positioned in a particular system than according to their individual personalities. Churches function in a similar manner. Relationships among churches are governed not on the basis of ability but on the basis of placement. We have discovered that one of the first principles of relationship is homeostasis (being in the same state). Once an ongoing network, system, or pattern of relating has been established, equilibrium forms. We have seen that this balance resists change, even when change is for the better. We want stability more than we want growth.

The Dent in the Hood

A second dynamic in the relational road is the **identified patient.** This term refers to the people we label as the sickest. This aspect of family systems teaches us not to be too quick in judging who the truly sick people are. The individuals with the most symptoms may not be the sickest. They may just be manifesting the illness of the whole system in themselves. These individuals could be compared to the dent in the hood of a car in which the run-off from a rainstorm ultimately collects.

Sometimes, the most sensitive and intelligent members of a broken family manifest the most problems. Every teacher knows that a child who acts up in the classroom may be the sweetest child in the family. The child may be reacting to the pain of divorce, abuse, or family illness. The other members of the family may be functioning fine, not because they are adjusted but because they are just so out of it.

When I was in seminary in Los Angeles, my wife, Carolyn, was working as an occupational therapist. She was completing her internship for locked-up schizophrenics at the Veteran's Affairs hospital. When she saw the unbelievable brokenness and emotional handicaps of these people, she asked the doctors how a human life could fall so far.

"These aren't the really sick ones," the doctors explained. "If you want to study illness, meet some of the parents who put them here."

Do you remember Typhoid Mary? She was a woman who carried the typhoid virus to hundreds, but she herself was immune to the symptoms. She felt fine, but she passed the illness to others who died. Some churches and communities feel just fine, but they are actually passing spiritual and relational illnesses on to others. Sick shepherds make sick sheep. We need to find the underlying reasons for disunity, not merely the presenting or obvious problems.

What we have tragically done in the past is to rush in too quickly and to focus on the problems of the neediest members in the body of Christ in a given city. While this is a noble venture, this is not the most effective method. As strange as it may sound, the best way to treat struggling Zion Baptist Church may be to come alongside St. John's Episcopal Church.

As we understand family systems, we will cease to obsess

about the symptoms we see in the most troubled individuals. Rather, we will learn to treat the system as a whole. The fantastic part is that we do not need the whole family/church present, nor do we need those people who have the worst problems present. To bring healing, we need to find the most *responsive* individuals.

We need to keep in mind that we are seeking to bring healing to the whole family of God in a given city. When the Apostle Paul wrote, "we are all members of one body" (Ephesians 4:25), he was doing more than fishing for illustrations. We are connected in a deeper way than any of us would dare to believe. As the various systems of our physical bodies are interrelated and affect each other, the same is true with our spiritual connectedness.

Every doctor knows that a problem affecting one system of the body can surface and can manifest a problem in a totally different system of the body. My father died of an aneurysm, a blown heart vein. Do you know what the doctor said was his primary problem? His kidneys. The renal system suffered a great trauma (he had only half a kidney); and that, in turn, put great stress on his circulatory system. One of my pastors has hepatitis C, a liver disease. Do you know how we know when the virus is more active? His skin turns yellow. One system's problem manifests itself in a different system.

When we truly grasp this, we will revolutionize our involvement with the rest of the body of Christ. The problems in the black church manifest themselves in the white church. The over-functioning suburban church forces the urban church to under function. Rather than asking, "Why can't those people ever get it together?" we should be asking, "What are we doing that unknowingly keeps them from getting it together?" Instead of asking, "Why don't those rich folks help us?" we should start asking, "What are we doing that keeps them from being able to share?"

It is in our vested self-interest to help every church in our city become as strong and healthy as possible. For the benefit of God's Kingdom? Of course! But, for our benefit, as well.

This does not mean that individuals should not assume responsibility for themselves. People are not helpless victims in an evil system. Jesus never asked systems to repent. He told individual people to repent. But, God did say time and time again in the Scriptures that we are to work toward just and loving systems in society. (Consider 2 Samuel 8:15, Micah 6:8, and Matthew 23:23.)

The thrust of this book is that it takes a regenerated heart to relate in a liberated way toward fallen relational networks. It would be easy to fall into the trap of a lost, secular evaluation. The world system tells us that our genes, society, and family histories create our behavior. This thinking is on the same level as saying that the trees move the wind. We must let the fresh wind of the Spirit fill and change our living relationships.

Reshaping the Focus

Once we understand that the person, the church, or the community with the most symptoms may not be the sickest one, we will refocus our attention. Our attention is no longer focused on fixing the problem at hand. It is focused on healing the relationship.

The power of God-gifted counselors is found not so much in their knowledge or in the techniques they use but in the quality of the relationships that they build with their clients. When counselors model healthy, non-manipulative relationships with hurting people, these people are in turn empowered to do the same with the relationships they are stuck in. When this happens with one person in a given family, even if the family system goes nuts and tries to punish or to woo the person into conforming, the entire system can be changed by this one responsive person. It is really God's healing hand brought into a sick family world.

The same is true in the church. When one brave person or, better yet, when one brave church decides to enter into a real relationship with a very entrenched or enmeshed association of churches, that one person or church can destabilize the iron grip of illness and then be used to foster authentic relationships.

Many identified patients carry ghosts from the past. "Emblem bearer" is a term for the children upon whom all the hopes, dreams, and identity of families lay. They are sent forth to conquer in the name of the family. When these chosen individuals fail, they feel that they have failed not only themselves but also the whole clan! (Tragically, many of today's suicide victims are family emblem bearers who felt they did not deserve to live.)

The suburban church should realize that many of the defensive and cocky attitudes of some of the urban churches come from the insecurities they hold in trying to purge this self-doubt that oppression brings. Some of these urban churches believe (unwisely) that they must succeed not just for themselves but for the whole African-American community. Remember, this is not a conscious thought process. It is the emotional reasoning we all work through. "I feel it; therefore, it must be true."

Furthermore, we cannot cure the problems of either the black or the white church apart from where these churches reside. Healing will not happen at a church conference or at a retreat. It would be as if we were taking a person's lungs out of his/her body and wondering why the lungs act differently on the table than when they are within the person's chest. This is about God's healing in wholeness. It is about bringing the power of God's presence in us into the everyday systems of another person or church.

A Question of Intentions

In ways, I fell into this mission of healing because at one time I was identified as the sick one. Although I do not know what it feels like to be a member of a racial minority, I do understand the stigma of being an outcast economically. Time spent with a pastor of another race helped me understand this.

"Brewer, what on earth ever made you start doing this? Just what is it you are really up to?"

That was a legitimate question, particularly, since it was coming from the vice president of the National Baptist Convention, the largest African-American organization in the country. This pastor of more than forty-five years had actually marched with Dr. Martin Luther King, Jr. Dr. Phillips had some great white friends over the years. He also knew some real cheesy dudes who were all about self-promotion and who were in no way brothers or sisters in the struggle. Dr. Phillips was not hesitant about getting to the bone of any issue.

I wondered myself. I was raised in a working-class, white family. Some of my immediate relatives could have been considered "white trash." They lived in cabins they had built in the mountains. A preacher's kid, I grew up in small towns and then moved to Denver before I finished grade school. My family was not openly racist. They were always kind to people. My grandparents told "colored people" jokes as many of that generation did. Was I trying to atone for their sins? No, it was not that. My sins were worse.

In high school, I hung out with black and Hispanic friends (Afro-American and Chicano then). We had some serious fights with blacks from other high schools, but we had fights with everyone. After high school, having given my life to Christ and having walked away from the party side of life, I drove a truck.

I would not say that teamsters was a great integrated experience, either.

"So, Brewer," Dr. Phillips asked me, "why are you so passionate about the relationship between the white and the black churches?"

Was it some great sense of guilt? Had I done some terrible evil against a person of color? No, it was not that.

Maybe, it was some indebtedness. Had some black man or woman helped in some profound way that I was trying to pay back? No, not that I could think of.

Maybe, it was a "wanna-be" syndrome. Did I really want to be accepted by blacks and be one of them? No, I love so much about the African-American church, people, and culture; but I actually like being white (even though at many of my meetings, I am the only one who is pigment-challenged).

Maybe, it was out of default because I could not make it in the super competitive league of suburbia; therefore, I went downtown where I could make a difference. No, God had humbly shown me that he could use me in suburbia. I saw two churches in my first twenty years of ministry grow from nothing to over seven thousand members, and I now lead an even larger suburban church. That was not it.

So, Brewer, why? Why have you for ten years given yourself to this crazy, unwinable, frustrating, no-glory mission? Do you have a martyr's complex or a Messianic illusion?

In answer to this pastor's question, I replied, "It may sound strange, but I owe Christ my life. He died for me. I know there are thousands of his servants more qualified than I, but I know he wants his children to love each other. I know what it is like to not fit in and to be on the economic outside looking in. It's an ache that eats your heart out. I also know that I have this bizarre hunger to build these relationships. I guess you could say I have self-interest. I know that if I pursue what God is pursuing, I receive the blessing. Besides, there doesn't seem to be a line right now of white pastors asking to spend their time in the black church. White churches either want to act like a black church, to have black people attend their white church, or to have black folks act like white folks. I want us to be who we are and to walk together. There's so much I don't know. I'm on a steep learning curve."

"Well, hang around, son," he encouraged. "I'm on a steep teaching curve."

Since that conversation in 1993, Dr. Phillips has become one of my true friends. Do we disagree? All the time. Do we frustrate each other? You bet. But, the intentions of the heart are present.

There is a difference between motives and intentions. Motives are always mixed in the human heart. When Jeremiah wrote, "The heart is deceitful above all things and beyond cure. Who can understand it?" (Jeremiah 17:9), he was saying that we all have good and bad motives. He was saying that if we are waiting to have nothing but pure motives before we move, we will never move.

Our intentions are the underlying reason and drive of the will. When I perform a wedding ceremony, I do not question the couple about their motives. For instance, I do not ask the groom, "What are your motives for taking this woman as your wife?" (He may have various motives.) Rather, I ask him about his intentions. "Will you have this woman as your wedded wife?" God holds us accountable for our intentions.

Let us be honest. Our motives are mixed for wanting the church to work together. What we must focus on are our intentions because it is our intentions that Christ asks us about. If our intentions are to honor him by loving our brothers and sisters, if our intentions are to share and to learn together for his glory, if our intentions are simply to let him work through us by his Spirit, then no demon in hell will stop us.

Summary

1. Another dynamic of family systems is the **identified patient.** The person with the most symptoms may not be the sickest puppy in the kennel. The most effective healing is not only to deal with the hurting church or community but also to ask who else within the system is malfunctioning and intensifying the illness.

2. The positive dimension of this is that we do not need to have everyone gathered in a room to fix each one. A system can be changed as we **empower the most responsive person** to create a healthy relationship with the others. Prayerfully, find the individuals, the church, or the prayer group within the given system and release them to be used by designing a new way of relating.

3. We all have mixed motives. God is concerned about our **underlying intentions.** We should not wait until all of our motives are pure. We must fan the flame of our hearts' intentions to serve Christ. It is a question of the will.

Chapter Five
Staying Differentiated

Differentiation

Leadership, according to family systems, is what Dr. Bowmen called **differentiation**. This term refers to the ability to stay in touch with others and to remain ourselves while others are screaming at us to be different. We stay calm no matter how anxious or how stressful the relationship becomes. Leadership is not about fixing problems or being a super motivator of others. It is all about being in the midst of the chaos and not allowing the toxic waste of the system to drip down inside of us. Often, in stressful situations, others want to pull us into "we thinking." "If you are really one of us, then you will do this or that." Others may also try to intimidate us into "you thinking." "My problem is now your problem. What are you going to do about it?" Differentiation is having the ability to stay fully "I" while staying in touch with the relationship.

Keeping on Course

The anger in the room was seething. The only Anglo in the room, I tried not to become caught between the two swelling waves of the old guard and the young, emerging leaders inside the African-American community. Along with ninety-nine per cent of suburbanites, I had no idea how large this rift had grown. Into what storm had my journey now led me? The scene was a luncheon. I had invited several pastors to discuss the scheduled stadium rally of Louis Farrakhan and the Nation of Islam. The dialogue intensified.

A young, frustrated black pastor paced as he vented some deep issues. "Mark, I honor what those men did for me. They are the men who actually walked with Dr. King during the worst of times. They are the men who as children were told to step off the sidewalk when a white person came their way. They remember "colored day" at the swimming pool. Dogs turned on them. Their relatives were beaten. They were forced to sit in the back of the bus. If it weren't for them, I could never have gone to school."

His passion grew, and he turned from me to the leaders up front. "But, I want to tell you something. These men have confused self-seeking politics and the Kingdom of God. All the times I attended their churches, with all the hooping and the hollering about Jesus, I never once was told how to give my life to Christ, not one time in sixteen years! The tactics of the 1960's are over! This is not about picketing and marching and 'pulling the racial card' every time someone crosses your little game. This is about Christ and his Kingdom, not ours!"

Several of the younger black men and women clapped and shouted, "Amen!" As he took his seat, silence engulfed the room.

One of the senior pastors in the room quietly stood up from his table. Every eye was on him. How was he going to respond? No one had dared to take on the movers and the shakers in public, at least not when they were seated together. He turned toward me.

"Our younger brother obviously has some issues he's dealing with." He slowly walked over to the young pastor. "Maybe, you don't like the way we do things. But, I'll bet you'd change your song if it were your kids who were being kicked around. Tell me something, Mister 'I-love-Jesus-more-than-any-of-you.' Do you know what it's like to have your children see you humiliated like an animal? To have them watch as you go to the back of the man's house because you'd better not go to the front? Do you know what it's like to knock on the porch door, keep your eyes down because you're not human enough to look the master in the eye, and hold out your hat for him to put in a few dollars for working his field? You naïve, sheltered fool! Don't kid yourself. They can take it away as fast as they give it. How dare you judge us! This is about God's Kingdom. It's about justice and dignity!"

The older pastors clapped and shouted all the louder. Then came the moment I will remember forever.

The senior pastor stared at me. "Dr. Brewer, what are you going to do about it?"

What?! What am I going to do about it? Surely, he was not referring to the super-charged wrestling match going on in front of me. Surely, he was addressing the question of who was to be the representative group to address Louis Farrakhan's planned trip to Denver. Right? My church had offered financial and volunteer support; and all I had asked was, "How would the African-American church in the city like to respond?"

My question had opened up the floodgate of strain between these two relational networks: the old, established guard and the young, upcoming leaders. I might as well have flown to the West Bank in Israel and asked a group of Jews and Arabs, "Hey, whose land is this?"

This meeting was about to become ugly. Then, I remembered one of the key powers of family systems. I replied, "Both of you have voiced deep and vital issues. I'm here today to help the churches in the city respond in a unified voice to this rising threat of Islam."

One of the younger women shouted, "That's right. This is about bringing people to Jesus. It's just that simple."

Then, one of the older pastors proclaimed, "The reason Farrakhan has any following is because the black church isn't taking care of our people's needs. The issues aren't theology. We know Christ is the only way. The real issues are drugs, violence, and self-respect for our children."

Both sides looked at me.

I responded, "I know that both of you want to keep your young people from following the Nation of Islam. You both want them to follow and to love the Lord. But, you're the ones to figure out, together, how to blend your vital concerns. I'm here to decide by next month whether to have our church stand by you at the rally for education or to stand by you at the evangelism and revival week. Maybe both."

The pastors did not suddenly rush across the room and embrace one another with loving hugs. They did, however, hang around, shake hands, and discuss more calmly how to help each other. No one changed anyone's mind that day. They did, however, change a keep-your-thoughts-to-yourself culture into a relationship of honesty.

Who was the winner that day? First, the church in Denver was a winner. Hearing that a city-wide unity in the black community was against him, Farrakhan never showed. Who was the second winner? I was. Why? I had, by God's grace, stayed in touch and defined the situation. It is what healing by leadership is all about.

Stay in Touch and Define

As stated earlier, family systems focuses on the problems

and the struggles of a given family system, rather than on the internal issues of the individual members. The healthiest person in a toxic relationship can become sick. The reverse is also true. A broken, diseased person placed in a healthy, loving network can be restored and renewed. The focus of healing is found in the relationships themselves, not in the separate pieces that make up the system. A leader knows how to keep from being pulled into other people's currents. Leaders fight like pit bulls to keep their boats on course. They do not fight the individual people involved. They resist the unconscious, relational waves.

In the Farrakhan situation, if I had let the waves push me into choosing between direct evangelism or practical help in Christ's Name or choosing between the older leadership and the up-and-coming leadership, I would have been sucked into an inescapable whirlpool. What I did was to focus my attention on my relationship with the entire group. As a leader, I stayed in touch and defined my relationship with the group. Do you remember the statement: You cannot help a relationship you are not in, and you cannot help a relationship you are stuck in? Leaders do not let others redefine the game. It is not a conspiracy; it is using the power of homeostasis and the pre-existing balance of the system.

Here is where we have a phenomenally effective asset on our side. It is the **power of presence**. We must not be pulled into "we" statements (which are unhealthy stuck statements) or, even worse, be pulled into "you" statements (which try to fuse others into our thinking). We need to let God bring his presence into the situation as we stay in touch and define. This requires using "I" statements. This is what "I" am about. This may seem like fancy footwork to avoid the real issues, but it is really the only effective tool for reconciliation.

Countless times, I have heard disgruntled church members ask, "Pastor, what are we going to do about this?" or "I don't know what you are going to do about so-and-so." The deeper issue is not about Mr. So-and-so; it is about my relationship with Mr. So-and-so. The healthy answer is a lot of "I" statements. We have been taught that "I" is self-centered. Much of the time it is. In leadership, however, if we truly love others as Christ loves others, we will lead by modeling a healthy, godly relationship.

A biblical relationship requires clear definition and staying on course. When I was involved with student ministry in Los Angeles, I learned a valuable lesson about escaping riptides. Riptides happen when waves approach the beach from two different angles. As a result, the flow of water back out to sea is enormously strong and fast. Unfortunately, a swimmer or a surfer cannot see this. The waves on the surface appear beautiful and predictable, but not so the currents underneath.

I was body surfing with the students when, suddenly, I felt my shorts being sucked to Japan! Naturally, I panicked and tried to swim to shore as hard as I could. The collegians were not laughing (which freaked me out even more because they were always laughing at me in the waves). They were yelling at me, telling me to stop swimming towards the shore and to start swimming down the side of the beach.

Obviously, I survived. But, I learned an important truth about undertows. The fastest way out is to swim parallel to the beach, not towards the beach. What? Do you reach the beach by not taking the shortest route? You bet. If you want to make it to shore, you have to swim out of the current first.

When churches (or any family system) try to come together, they can create huge relational riptides. Why? People, like the waves at the beach, often come together from two different angles. How do we keep from becoming sucked into irresolvable issues that keep relationships from building? The answer is simple. We must keep in touch and define. Simple, yes, but not easy.

Sometimes, the clearest way to see an object is to look to the side of it. When we look at objects in the dark, our eyes do not stare directly at these objects. Our eyes actually look cockeyed at objects in the dark. On the outside of the back of our eyes are cells called rods. These cells see only black and white. Located directly on the back of our eyes are other cells called cones. These pick up the color. Since the rods pick up black and white only, when we are trying to see in the dark, our heads automatically adjust by looking to the side of the object in order to let in the little bit of black and white light. (Since cats and owls have only rods in their eyes, they see well at night.)

Just as we see objects better in the dark by looking to the side of them; sometimes, the best way to see what is actually going on with a relationship is to look to the side of it. We need to stop and to watch the currents between people. It is quite revealing.

Our Lord's Masterful Ability to Define

On countless occasions, we find Christ's enemies trying to trap him in theological riptides. Jesus was a master of family systems. (It is probably because he is the Master!) Recall the time the Pharisees tried to trap him on the issue of giving taxes to Rome (Matthew 22:15-22). They were sure they had him cornered because the people hated Rome. If Jesus said, "Yes, pay taxes to Rome," the Pharisees could portray him as a hypocritical traitor to Israel who supported those pig-eating, Gentile conquerors. But, if he said, "No way should you pay taxes to Rome," then they could convict him as a treasonous rebel to Rome. Talk about an inescapable riptide.

Yet, Jesus did not take the bait. He delegated the anxiety back to the Pharisees. "Bring me a coin," he replied. "Whose image is on it? Then give to Caesar what is Caesar's, and give to God what is God's." The game was over.

Someone might say, "But, Jesus never answered the question." Yes, he did in two ways. First, Jesus said that we have a responsibility to both government and to God. Second, and more importantly, he delegated the anxiety back to others. He swam out of the undertow by defining that he was not about solving people's relationships with their enemies. In essence, he said, "I can't live your life for you. I will live my life and relationship with you. You have to make your own decisions about your life."

Family systems revolutionized my understanding about leadership. Leadership is not having all the right answers to the enormously complex problems that plague our world. Leadership is our position in systems and how we respond to others. As we take Christ's hand and engage in authentic relationships, while lovingly and clearly defining who we are, we will find that we can wade into the stickiest situations and not become stuck. By modeling a loving and liberating way of relating, others are healed and are set free to be themselves, as well.

It is precisely this power of being that Dr. Friedman called a **non-anxious presence**. Developing this style of leadership allows God to use us in remarkable ways. To be a non-anxious presence, we need to be present in the lives of others and to be actively engaged in their lives. We also need to be non-anxious. This does not mean non-nervous. Rather, to be leaders, we must be careful not to absorb or to try to resolve the anxiety present in the relational system. We dare not own what is not ours.

Stress, seen in this light, does not have to do with the problem. It has to do with our relationship to the problem. Some people weather hurricane-force storms, and others sink with a few waves. It is not because of their boats or the waves. It is all about how they are relating to their boats and to the waves. We can go through enormous storms and not sink if we keep from being sucked into the storm.

When our relationship to a problem changes, likewise, our emotional stress changes. Have you ever noticed how differently people feel about a sporting event when they have bet money on the game? The game has not changed, but the relationship between these individuals and the game has.

When I first started sharing in the meetings of some African-American churches, I was really tense. It was not because I was new. It was because I thought (wrongly) that they would not accept me unless I could fix some of their problems. The more I owned emotionally, the more emotionally exhausted I became. I was always offering to help, and they gladly accepted my help. (By the way, if you do not constantly define what you are about, others will do it for you.) The inevitable effect was to become so exhausted that I was walking away saying, "I can't take it anymore. I just can't solve these problems." I was doing the opposite of healthy family systems. I was owning what was not mine to own, and I was letting others define what my relationship was about. This is so different from what Jesus would do.

Consider this example recorded in John 8:2-11. While our Lord was teaching in the temple courts, the teachers of the Law and the Pharisees set him up once again. These religious leaders had caught a woman having sex with a man to whom she was not married. The religious leaders threw her into the middle of Jesus' class and questioned him. "In the Law Moses commanded us to stone such women. Now, what do you say?" (verse 5). Another inescapable trap, so these leaders thought. If Jesus said, "Yes, kill her. She's a sinner," then those who followed him because of his acceptance, forgiveness, and grace would leave this cold-hearted legalist. But, if Jesus said, "No, don't hurt her," then he was saying that what Moses had said did not matter.

Jesus' response was obviously not what these enemies were expecting. He delegated the anxiety and the problem back to them. "If any one of you is without sin, let him be the first to throw a stone at her," he replied (verse 7). He affirmed the woman's wrong behavior; and then, according to custom, the one sinned against or the most righteous should begin the punishment. These religious leaders said nothing and cowered away one at a time.

Jesus was not pulled into debating the law, and he was not pulled into the woman's life. He did not rescue his enemies from honest, self-appraisal. Neither did he rescue the woman from her responsibilities; for he told her, "Go now and leave your life of sin" (verse 11). He simply defined what he was about and let them decide their own issues.

I would have tried to rescue one of them. Am I so loving? No, I have a low threshold for others' pain.

Raising Our Threshold for Other People's Pain

We all know that to get in shape physically, we must raise our threshold or our limit of pain. If we want to see our strength increase, we must push our muscles until they hurt. Similarly, if we want to learn to play a musical instrument, we must endure the drudgery of practicing scales and notes. Why? It is only when we discipline ourselves that we will be able to achieve higher levels.

Some of us have children to raise, and our focus shifts from ourselves to them. We start dealing with how our beloved children deal with frustration and with pain. We refrain from rescuing our children when they throw a tantrum because we want them to grow and to mature. Parents who cannot stand to hear their children rant and complain about having to do chores will have aided in stopping their children's development. As parents, we must raise our threshold for their pain. This is not being mean. On the contrary, it is what love is all about. Since we desire their highest welfare, we must let them work through their own struggles.

Every teacher knows that giving a student an undeserved grade does not help that young person succeed later in life. Instead, it dooms that student. Although it is tough at times to watch, teachers must raise their threshold for their students' pain. Nothing can replace the sheer joy of hearing a child say, "I can do it!"

Similarly, coaches know not to let athletes quit simply because excelling is tough. Coaches will assist, encourage, and support. They will raise their threshold for the athlete's pain to see this athlete triumph.

Christ modeled what leadership within churches should look like. He did not ignore or refuse to help a hurting person, but neither did he go about solving that person's problem without involving that person in some way. Leadership, according to family systems, requires that we stay in touch and define what we should and should not do to help others. Leaders must find the right place to stand in a given relational network, and they must let God be God.

One Difference between Heaven and Hell

The stunning irony about this kind of leadership is that the more we help people help themselves, the more we help ourselves. When we talk about being an answer to the prayer of Christ in the garden, "that all of them may be one, Father, just as you are in me and I am in you. May they also be in us so that the world may believe that you have sent me" (John 17:21), we are living out two remarkable truths. The first truth is that the world has the right to decide if Jesus is who he said he is based on how we love each other. How do you think Jesus feels about the reputation we have given him? I grow very nervous when I honestly think about it. The other great truth is that heaven is giving. The Bible tells us, "God is love" (I John 4:8). The more we live according to God's commands, the greater our lives become. The more we live for our own little fiefdoms and territories, the more empty and miserable our lives become. In his book, *The Problem of Pain,* C.S. Lewis wrote, "Heaven will be where we say to God, 'Thy will be done.' Hell will be where God says to the rebels, 'Thy will be done.'"

I am reminded of a story about a gentleman who found himself at the gates of eternity. Seeing that the man's debts had been fully paid by Christ, the gatekeepers welcomed him and ushered him into heaven. The gentleman realized it was an unusual request but asked if he might have a peek at what the other place was like. The gatekeepers left for a moment, came back, and granted his request.

In a flash, he was in the place of the damned. Moaning, cursing, and wailing filled the air. When he peered into a great ballroom, he saw emaciated, starving people with piles of luscious food placed before them. They all had one arm tied behind their backs and a two-foot-long spoon tied to their other arm. Watching, he saw that they tried in vain to put the food in their own mouths. Inevitably, the food fell off the spoon, and they screamed and cursed. They would never die, but they would be eternally hungry.

"Quick," he said, "take me from here!"

At once, he was taken to his home in glory where he heard singing, laughing, and praise. He entered another grand ballroom. The set up was the same. People were seated all around. Delicious food was piled in front of everyone. Everyone had one arm tied behind their backs and a long spoon tied to their other arm. But, these people were full, super healthy, and dripping with joy. What made the difference? They were feeding each other!

We all have the ability to feed from the King's table. The more we lead by knowing who we are, the more we will serve those next to us.

Summary

1. All too often in stressful situations, people in the church will try to pull us into their own issues. This is not done consciously. It is a natural response to stress. The ability to **stay differentiated is the key to healing by leadership**. The more sickly fused or welded a relational network is, the greater the tendency will be to have an "us-vs.-them" thinking. We must not let our boat be pulled off course. The answer is to keep in touch and to define. Although others may continually ask us, "Well, what about this issue?" or "What about that group?" we need to simply keep in touch and to tell them what we are about.

2. The **power of presence is allowing God to fill us with himself in a given relational system**. This involves delegating other people's anxieties back to them. Jesus did it, and we can too. This does not mean that we have an I-don't-care attitude. Quite the opposite is true. When we delegate the anxiety back, we are saying, "How can I help you deal with your life?" It is the height of spiritual pride to think that we can live others' lives. It is the depth of spiritual stubbornness not to help.

3. Just as parents, teachers and coaches, we must resist the urge to rescue. Instead, we must **raise our threshold for another person's anxiety**. Urban churches do not have to fix suburban emptiness. Suburban churches cannot solve all the brokenness in the inner cities. We must take the hand of Christ and each other's to gain the victory in our shared world.

Chapter Six
What Peter Tells You about Paul

A nervous excitement filled the air. For many of the pastors in the room, this was the first time they had ever crossed such radical lines. We could feel the energy and God's presence. Most churches think they are global if they just interact with another church from their own denomination. This gathering included the whole church zoo. There were Pentecostals, Presbyterians, Baptists, Brethren, Charismatics, Catholics, Messianic Jews, Orthodox Arabs, African-Americans, Hispanics, Asians, Anglos, old, young. You name it, and they were there!

This was the last meeting at the arena before the great gathering in two weeks. Everything, except a few final decisions about who was doing what on the platform the night of the praise event, was set. Everything was going well until I was ambushed by the dynamic called "sabotage." A well-known pastor stepped to the microphone during lunch. He had a large church and an important ministry in the city. As he had been taking a beating from some of the other pastors in town, I figured it was, as penned by Shakespeare in *Othello,* "the green-eyed monster of jealousy raising its ugly head."

"We all appreciate what Mark has done to help put this together. But, we also know that most of us have been left out of the decision making. I guess what is said about the golden rule is true: The one with the gold makes the rules."

I almost dropped my burrito. I looked around the room; and, sure enough, my nametag was the only one with "Mark" written on it. If I had not known a little about family systems, I would have blasted the guy; but that would have played into a triangle that was trying to materialize.

I responded, "Brother, it sounds like you're a bit sarcastic. It sounds as though you're a little hurt that you weren't asked to lead."

He laughed, "No, I was just kidding." Then, he pulled me aside as the others tried to resume eating. "Mark, I just want you to know that I said that because so many are already saying it. I'm trying to defend you all the time. But, oh, well, let's just let it pass."

Right. Letting it pass would be like letting a cancer diagnosis just pass. I approached the podium; and in the most calm and open voice possible, I inquired, "Brothers and Sisters, does anyone feel that I've been running over you?" The room was silent.

I turned to Pastor Sabotage. "Could you tell me who they are?"

"No," he said. "It was told to me in confidence." (I love that about the church. Confidence means just telling one person at a time.)

"Well," I replied, "if anyone has any problems, we must bring them out now. Otherwise, let's get on with our mission and watch God move!" Everyone applauded and went on dining.

What had just happened was more than a cheap shot by a jealous, scorned pastor. What had happened was one of the most common reactions to tension and stress that a system ever encounters. It is called **triangling**.

Triangling - The Church's Favorite Sport

If we are to be used by God to help bring the church together, we must understand triangles. Any three persons or issues form a triangle. Why do they form? Any time two people are anxious or tense with each other, they will bring in a third party to try to deflect the tension, thus, keeping the balance (homeostasis) between the two of them.

For example, two lumberjacks holding onto each other while slipping off a log will grab a third person in order to maintain their balance to avoid falling into the water. That is triangling.

Do you remember the Arab saying, "The enemy of my enemy is my friend"? Triangling is the system's process of creating a necessary enemy for the purpose of stabilizing a shaky relationship.

We triangled in grade school. Do you remember being nervous around a cute member of the opposite sex? We said some silly put-downs about someone else in order to calm the situation.

Our political system is built upon this same gamesmanship. Both Republicans and Democrats are constantly pointing out the most recent boogey man we as allies are against. Diversion is in our relational bones.

Let us look back at the opening example. Some of the tactical language by the pastor who was trying to triangle me are textbook examples. The essence of the statement is this: "They're saying mean things about you because they're your enemy. I'm saying good things about you because I'm your friend." Those who have not had a little family-systems knowledge would have taken the bait and gone after the supposed issue.

In responding to triangles, we need to look at the *process* more than the content. Most people dive head long into the package they have been delivered. Systems understanding focuses on the vehicle that delivered the cargo as much as on the package itself.

Dr. Friedman pointed out, "What Peter tells you about Paul has more to do with you and your relationship to Peter, than anything about Paul." We need to ask ourselves, "Why is this person telling me this, now? What is the threat or anxiety?" (We need to remember, however, that not everything is driven by anxious behavior. People who are at peace with the relationship and who love us simply tell us things. We cannot become hyper about every statement. If we keep pulling up a plant to check on the roots, we will kill it. There are times to just let the plant be and allow it to grow.) We need to train ourselves to listen to relationships as much as to information.

Realize, also, that triangling is not some deceptive, thought-out scheme. It is as unconscious as the reflexes in our bodies.

Sabotage and Seduction

How are we pulled into triangles? The web of relational triangles has two basic threads, sabotage (the push me-pull you) and seduction. Once we understand this triangling game, we can become as agile in dodging these lassos as others are in throwing them.

The first force in causing others to behave for the system is known as **sabotage**. Sabotage is simply the act of threatening others if they even think of changing the status quo. We have all experienced the game of sabotage; and, sadly, we have all used it. For instance, your dog breaks free from the leash and races down the street. In response, you threaten your dog by yelling, "If you don't come back here, I'll never take you on a walk again!"

Here are several other examples: A parent threatens to disinherit a child if the child refuses to act or respond as the parent wishes. A white church threatens to cut off money to a black church if the black church does not vote the way the white church votes. A black church threatens to publicly shame a white church by picketing if the white church will not give the black church what it needs.

Does it work? You bet it does! But, what it really does is to keep the system entrenched so that authentic relationships become harder to build. We must be very careful how we relate to each other on today's big issues. Winning and losing have little to do with politics, the doctrine of the Holy Spirit, or economics. Winning and losing have much to do with how we relate to each other.

Notice, that this relational policing action that threatens the system is called sabotage, not attacking. Why? Only an outside enemy can truly attack. Someone on the inside must plant the bomb of sabotage because it is confined to an already established relationship. The balance, or homeostasis, has to already exist. It is true that outside systems can bully, threaten, intimidate, and coerce; but the power of sabotage is that it comes from someone inside that we think has our interests at heart. Otherwise, we would simply blow off that person. When we have a relational covenant with the source, the threat of sabotage has the real power to control our behavior.

When we are married, we do not just marry our lover. We marry our lover's whole family. If you do not believe me, think back to the first extended family meal with your honey at Thanksgiving or Christmas. The triangling that occurred at that gathering shamed any two sheep dogs driving home a lost sheep.

With everyone rushing to the altar to join together in ministry marriage, imagine all the triangles that are swirling around. We simply need to open our relational eyes and to take some mental notes to see triangling happening. Be assured, just as we are pulled into family triangles when we marry, the gravity of church triangles will try to suck us in, as well.

The other thread in the web of triangles that keeps people who are systems disruptive in line is called **seduction**. Whereas, sabotage plays to the fear part of our nature (no one wants to be voted most disliked or to be banished from the group), seduction plays to the nurturing and rescuing side of our nature. "You're so great. Won't you help me?" or "Now you've done it. Watch me die and my blood be on your hands." Sabotage is the appetizer of church triangles; seduction is the main meal.

Since it is very hard to stand aside and watch someone go under the water (even if you know it is probably staged), the game of seduction has such a target-rich environment in the church. We are supposed to be willing to lie down and to die for our brothers and sisters. Differentiation becomes crucial at this point. We need to understand that we are to die for our brother's and sister's good, not for some entrenched system. Christ calls us to live for his Kingdom, not a stuck institution.

In a family, the passive-aggressive mother uses seduction when she laments, "You never come to see me. I so love seeing you. It makes my day. But, I know you're busy. I'll just die alone rather than be a burden to you." There is no threat to this tactic. It is all about playing to the vanity and rescuing guilt of another human being.

Do you see why it has been mastered by those in the church? Just as strong churches use threats to modify behavior within, weak churches use seduction to pull misbehaving churches in the city into line. Handcuffs, such as, "Would a loving follower of Jesus let us go under?" or "You've meant so much to us," or

"It must be nice to have such a large congregation and all that money," are common ropes.

Often, seduction is the unseen weapon of the poorer black church used against the unseen weapon of sabotage of the wealthier white church. Of course, these neutral tactics work just as well in the other group's arsenal. The whole point is that we can learn to objectively see what is going on and to objectively resolve to use it to create a healthier relationship.

Detrianglers and Other Equipment for the Journey

The paradox of play and the art of stepping back are the two most effective tools for escaping the entanglement of newly formed triangles. I have discovered that I am great at one and a disaster with the other.

The paradox of play is merely the open refusal to treat the triangle in a serious way. The power of humor or jesting is deep in every culture. Having studied humor, I have found that it is, basically, a way of devaluing. Notice that jokes, in an absurd way, are about painful situations. From slapstick to television sit-coms, everyday stresses are played out and devalued. That is their appeal. Have you ever thought about why you hate being part of a practical joke? You are the object of someone else's devaluing. Using the paradox of play to escape triangling, the other person or the issue is never devalued. It is the game of the system that is not taken seriously. Humor can be misused when treating people, the mission, or Christ in a flippant or demeaning manner. I am not talking about that. That is as far from play as it can be.

Playfulness happens when we attempt to control the steam without defending ourselves. I cannot tell you the number of times I have used this. (I do have to be careful because my natural joking style can be misread.) For example, a woman came up to me and remarked, "Pastor, those sermons are getting a little stale." I simply replied, "I hope you buy the tapes so you can sleep at night." Here is another example: "I wish I only had to work one day a week." My response, "One day? I only work one morning!" We reply in such a manner that we refuse to be pulled into a confrontation.

When we refuse to struggle for control, we will be detriangling. A person called the church office and asked, "Is the pastor there?" The receptionist answered, "No, he's not." The caller replied, "Oh, he must be out spreading more lies!" The receptionist refused the challenge and calmly said, "No, today is his day off."

This is not about clever one liners. It actually has very little to do with language. It is about defining and staying in touch as we let the pitches of control roll out into center field and consciously choose never to pick them up. A world of difference exists when I am at a heated meeting about white churches or black churches and the paradox of play has come in. Trying to be cute always backfires. People know when others are saying they or their issues are a joke. That is fighting words! But, when we refuse to take the bait of relational confrontation, we strangely sidestep the game. People slink away a little confused and dazed when we treat their game of triangling playfully and refuse, at least on the surface, to take it seriously.

The other tool to possess in our healing bag is the ability to step back. I did not say step out, just step back. Trying to bring two anxious systems together through relationship is akin to grabbing two cut ends of an electrical wire in each hand. If we offer, the voltage will graciously pass through our bodies; and we will fry!

A disrupted or unstable relational system will always unconsciously look for a bridge to walk over. In stepping back, we help build up the people who will bridge themselves, and we refuse to be the highway they drive over. Why? The harder we try to bring two conflicting parties together, one of two actions results. We either keep them further apart, or we end up keeping the tension and the anxiety of the relationship in our heads.

At first, I thought I could help bridge the gap between the African-American church and the Anglo churches I knew. The problem was that I was the only relational common denominator between them.

At one time, I decided that I would bring the leadership of my church and the leadership of another church together. Since tension resulted in a previous attempt, I felt we needed to sit down to talk. We sat down, introduced ourselves, and shared our personal challenges and past frustrations. Then, one of the well-meaning elders from my church asked if there was anything our church could do for their church. (The phrase, "our church," can be best translated, Dr. Brewer.) Before I knew it, in one Saturday morning, I had inherited the refurbishing of a downtown building!

We need to keep our relational glasses on. If the issue had simply been delegating a construction project, that could have been easily passed on. The real issue was that these two churches were extremely uncomfortable with each other, and I was the triangled-in comforter. How did I know that? The months that followed proved it. When I sent over a construction team, both churches went a little crazy if I was not present. Did they really think I was such a great craftsman that my skill was needed? Hardly. I realized that I had failed to handle the most important piece of the building project. I had failed to delegate the anxiety of relating back to the system. As soon as I realized what was going on, I asked two of the influential leaders what their plans were for resolving this. After several weeks of playing sabotage and seduction games, the men's groups from both churches went on one of the best retreats they had ever had. I stayed in touch and defined.

The more aware we are of the emotional rules and the relational processes, the more prepared we will be to finish our mission as opposed to just start it. There are no awards for winning the first two miles of a marathon. No one receives a trophy for the score at halftime. God is concerned about how we finish the race, not how enthusiastically we start it.

I want to finish my journey into the African-American community. I have so much more to learn and to share. I know fellow black pastors who want to eagerly journey into white suburbia. Understanding triangles will give all of us a great jump into the journey.

The Strength of Synergy

In the 1980's, management and business fell in love with the word "synergy." In mathematics, the term means that the whole is more than the sum of the parts. In a sense, it means that two plus two equals five. A family of four is more than just a man, a woman, and two smaller versions. An added strength is present. As these four people are in relationship, their combined strengths are greater than their individual strengths. If applied to cooking, synergy is the flavor of a stew. When cooking a stew, the meat does not become carrots, and the potatoes do not become peas. But, when mixed together, they all take on a unique flavor beyond the ingredients used. The way they blend together makes the difference. There is a spooky power when we work together rather than alone.

I was reading about a horse-pulling contest that took place several years ago in the Midwest. Farmers from miles around brought their huge draft horses to see which one could pull the most weight. These beautiful beasts were harnessed to a sledge with rocks stacked on top. Slowly, the competition weeded out the horses as the judges added more weight to the sledge. It finally came down to two Clydesdales. The winner pulled two thousand pounds, and the runner-up pulled eighteen hundred pounds. Everyone clapped and congratulated Farmer Jones for his fine horse. Then, someone suggested that the horses be hooked together to see if they could pull four thousand pounds. Everyone thought the strength of the winner would motivate the runner-up to pull more. The farmers harnessed the two horses together and loaded up the sledge. The result? Together, they pulled an astonishing six thousand pounds! The physical synergy of working along side each other far surpassed anything these horses could do alone.

The church is no different. The greatest force on earth is Jesus' church working together. We must harness ourselves together in healthy, creative ways so that the yoke of our Master really does make the burden light for the long haul (Matthew 11:29,30).

Summary

1. One of the most common ways to handle stressful relationships is **triangling.** Triangling occurs when two people who are uncomfortable with each other pull in a third person or issue to try to divert the anxiety. "What Peter tells you about Paul is really about you and Peter, nothing about Paul." If we are going to build relationships between such deep and old systems as the black and the white church, we must be ready for major-league triangling. It is not a plot. It is a system trying to find the old balance that we have upset.

2. Two of the tactical hooks that triangles use are **sabotage** and **seduction**. Sabotage is the inside threat element of keeping others from changing the system for fear of being punished. Seduction plays to the rescuing and nurturing side

of our nature. It is the flattering, "You're so great, so don't let my blood be on your hands," game.

3. Two handy tools to avoid being triangled into an anxious system are **the paradox of play** and **stepping aside**. The paradox of play refuses to take confrontation seriously. It is not about using humor or mocking the person or issue to deflect confrontation. Rather, it is not letting the seriousness of the triangle form. Side stepping is similar and focuses on not becoming the glue that tries to bring two parties together. The harder we try to make people relate, the further we keep them apart. Why? We keep them from having to relate to each other.

Chapter Seven
Unseen Players -The Extended Family

Background Radiation

Numb, I stared at my brother's body in the casket. Apart from my wife, no one was closer to me than he. God had gifted Tim incredibly. He was an all-conference athlete in high school and the first person in my family to letter in more than one sport. A member of five honor societies, he achieved a 4.0 grade point average throughout his college and graduate studies. His sense of humor would make Alan Greenspan split his side. Tim had started and organized a church in Michigan, then pastored two large, historical Presbyterian churches in Los Angeles and St. Louis. He had a beautiful wife and three children whom he loved dearly. He had survived mountain-climbing accidents and car wrecks. His courage endured when one of his legs had to be amputated. Within several weeks of the surgery, he was back in the pulpit with his contagious smile and zest for life. Five months later, Tim committed suicide. With so much going for him, what made him choke the life out of himself by breathing in car fumes in his garage?

I have wrestled a number of times with the "why" question because Tim was not the first casualty in my family. The brutality of the ministry had claimed others. My father had built one of the fastest growing churches in the city. At the zenith of its growth, my dad left our family and the ministry and married his secretary. I was seventeen years old at the time and had just given my life to the Lord. Needless to say, it was hard to connect the dots. Since that time, my spiritual father left his wife of thirty-five years, as well as his church. Another friend of many years, a young and gifted pastor who stood by me at our ordination, shot his wife in the neck with a thirty-eight special and then killed himself. There are others. What is going on?

Are these people just weaker than we are? No. Is it that they are not as talented, called, or spiritually blessed as we are? Hardly. Then, what on earth is going on? The answer lies in one common thread. At the time of each of their disasters, they were living in a relational system that had interlocked around them.

Our lives are not as water tight as we would like them to be. We all live in a number of emotional and relational networks, simultaneously. We belong to the family we were born into, the family we married into (which includes our spouse's family network), and the family of our local congregation (which is every bit as powerful as our biological family).

When I consider the tragic choices made by my brother, father, and friends, I realize that none of them was a passive victim. I now see with hindsight that each had deep issues in several relational networks that were colliding at the same time. Tornadoes and hurricanes happen when the elements of heat, wind, and barometric pressure intersect at the same time. Alone, these three elements are harmless. When they arrange at the same time, the storm breaks loose.

If we seriously plan to hook up with other congregational families across racial lines, we must learn this fact. People from our past and the present hold a gravitational pull on us. As we understand the extended family network, we can understand why some people flare up at the times they do. Racial strains calmly addressed at one time can blow up in our faces at another time. The issues have not changed, but the relational ecosystems around them have.

Unseen forces exist that we need to take into account. The people we are involved with have relationships we do not see, but these relationships are definitely adding to the stew. The explosions of unresolved conflicts in one system can vent themselves into another system. For example, a fight at home can fuel a fight at the office or at the church. The chilly way a church leader responds toward our efforts to help may have nothing to do with us. Issues in another relational network in that leader's life may be in turmoil.

Unseen Players on the Field

I recall a time in high school when we were playing a summer football scrimmage against a rival school. My team sat in stunned disbelief at the stamina of the opposing team's players. At the start of the fourth quarter, they were as fresh as they were at kick off. Later, we found out why. As a joke, they had brought starters from other schools into the locker room. Unknown to us, every time one of the guys went in to use the bathroom, a different player came out with the same jersey. Not only were they fresh, but also they were calling plays in the huddle that our defense had never seen.

I know a man who was marrying the woman of his parents' dreams, not the woman of his own dreams. The trouble was that the relational system of his biological family was the most frozen and stuck, and the real nightmare was that the bride and her children were unaware of what was driving his decision. The family system of his biological family of origin was strongly influencing the new family network of his wife and her children. Unseen players were involved in the love affair.

The same can be true within church families. The unseen forces of other relational systems can be pushing and pulling the people we are dealing with in all sorts of bizarre directions. When we marry into a new church across racial lines, we are marrying that church's whole family of relationships. We do not need to be afraid of these unseen currents; we just need to be educated. As we learn to heal and to differentiate in one network, we will help transform the other networks we are in.

Because the dynamics and the forces of families are the same, whether these families are African-American, Anglo, Hispanic, or Asian, we can see that cultures are different; but people are the same. The basic principles and dynamics of our biological families are the same as those of our spiritual church families. The teams may change jerseys, but the game is primarily the same. This gives those who are educated in the family-systems game a tremendous advantage in the spiritual struggle for unity in the body of Christ.

We can really see very little into the lives of others. We often forget that how they are relating to us is in response to how they are relating to others. I had a friend who drove a cattle rig for a living. He hated it. It was not because of the low pay or the smell of the animals. He disliked it because it was much more draining to haul several tons of cattle than to haul several tons of cargo. Why? Cattle do not stand still. The weight in the trailer was constantly shifting. Depending on what those crazy cows were doing determined how the rig handled. When we enter into honest relationships with other racial churches, we need to keep in mind that more players exist than the ones we see on the field. We all have shifting cows in the trailers of our families.

When another group is reacting strangely toward us, we should whisper a prayer for discernment and for insight as to what is happening in their other networks. It will save us a lot of wasted energy and worry. [The statement, "We have no idea the crosses that people are carrying," is so true. Jesus told us not to judge (Matthew 7:1) because we do not have the inside data on other people's lives. We have no concept of the daily burdens folks around us carry. We need to leave the judging to Jesus. Otherwise, we will end up punishing the victim and rewarding the criminal. Only God knows a person's heart.]

In-house Preaching

African-Americans entering into a suburban church network should remember that much of the in-house talk they hear is not directed at them. Innumerable times, I have heard white folks ranting and raving about big government and the need to bring some morality and freedom back into our country. They say that the bleeding-heart, liberal churches downtown care only about avoiding responsibility. Do they believe it? Mostly. To whom are they talking? The people in their own pews. Often, this is about reinforcing an insecure relationship among themselves.

Again, I do not want to say that these suburban churches do not believe in the issues they are so wound up about. What I am saying is that we must learn to hear the relational debate behind the social topic of the hour. It is not unusual for them to be unconsciously proving that they are Bible-believing evangelicals. Why? Many times their in-house relationships are anxious or threatened, and they triangle in an outside issue. It is not that suburbia does not passionately believe in hard work, morality, and freedom. It is just that, often, there are stronger currents under the surface. (My father, who served in the Navy, said that sometimes a strange phenomenon happens with icebergs. Icebergs can actually be spotted moving against the waves. What is the reason? The currents under the surface are stronger than the currents on the surface.)

Anglos who attend the Martin Luther King, Jr. celebration will hear the litany of evils that the whites have done. As the white racist culture is berated and statements are made, such as "I never met a white man or woman who didn't want to keep the black man down," rather than becoming defensive and walking out (sometimes my church members do), Anglos may want to put on their relational glasses. Sometimes, the issues are unconsciously cloaking an in-house relationship issue.

I am not saying that the volatile issues of racism in America are not accurate and in need of repentance. What I am trying to communicate to those of us who are really going to go deep into this reconciliation journey is that other forces are at work.

Remember the phrase, "the enemy of my enemy is my friend"? I have personally been in meetings where the speaker said they would rather be beaten than shake the hand of a white man only to have the speaker take me out for pie afterwards. Is this hypocrisy? Is this wishy-washy schizophrenia? No. This is the dynamics of the extended family. It was for the benefit of those in the house, not for the white visitor.

It resembles being invited to my in-laws' house for supper. My wife acts differently at her parents' home. We all do. It is not an integrity issue. It is an issue of homeostatic forces in two relational systems that happen to overlap. We need to listen to what is being said with an element of mature objectivity.

The Home Field May Not Be to Our Advantage

I have a favorite Chinese restaurant that I frequent. One employee always bugged me. The cashier was one of the meanest, most obnoxious people I had ever met. She did more to drive away business than the restaurant's great food did to bring in business. Why on earth did they keep her? The reason was simple. She was the grandmother. Honoring the elderly, particularly in one's family, was of greater social value in the Chinese system than honoring the customer. We may wonder why people do what they do. It appears so counter productive, that is, until we see the players off stage in their relational worlds.

Jesus knows about the game of the extended family. He knows that the benign cancer of sick relational networks is attacking us poor souls who are lost and trapped in a sin-filled, fallen world.

In Matthew 16, in a curious use of relational dynamics, Jesus asked his disciples, "Who do people say the Son of Man is?" (verse 13). Now, the Son of God did not need the boys to inform him about the talk on the street. He was seeing if they were being triangled into the assumptions about him. He was keeping in touch. Then, Jesus asked, "But what about you? Who do you say I am?" (verse 15).

Peter jumped to his feet and exclaimed, "You are the Christ, the Son of the living God!" (verse 16).

Jesus replied, "Peter, I know you. You did not come up with this on your own. My Father revealed this to you" (*my paraphrase,* verse 17). Then, Christ defined his relationship with Simon. "You are Peter," which means rock, "and on this rock I will build my church" (verse 18).

Peter's confession, as well as his life, would be crucial to Christ. It was a great day. Right? It was until Jesus spoke of his coming crucifixion and resurrection. Then, Peter tried to talk Christ out of going to the cross. "I'll never let this happen," Peter argued. "We have a good thing going" (*my paraphrase,* verse 22).

Satan is so shrewd (or are we just so naïve), for he uses the ones closest to us to discourage us the most. Yet, Jesus refused to take the bait. Addressing Peter, he commanded, "Get behind me, Satan! You do not have in mind the things of God, but the things of men" (verse 23).

Christ knew the power of these living organisms we call friendships and family relationships. They really do take on a life of their own. Jesus never let others define who he was or what he was about. For the sake of my salvation, I am glad! He, like any of us traveling into another culture, must know what it is we are not about as much as what we are about. I have had to get back on course continually. The relational currents are strong. It is so good to know that the Master understands.

On another occasion, a man in a gathering crowd asked Jesus to settle a legal and economic issue. What was Jesus' reply? "Who appointed me a judge or an arbiter between you?" (Luke 12:14). Someone may question, "I thought Jesus was the Judge of all?" He is. What he meant was that he was not going to be pulled into the side currents of their extended families. The fight was over land, which in Palestine was always family based. Christ Jesus was, in essence, saying, "Here is my relationship with you. What are you going to do with that? You handle your other relationships as honestly and as openly as you do your relationship with me."

Someday, the struggle will be over. Our relationships will be healed, renewed, and transformed (as will be the rest of God's new earth and heaven). The bride will be ready. The relationships we think are the most intimate and precious now will seem like pen pals compared to our relationships in heaven. Our job, in the mean time, is to cooperate by preparing for that day.

I have learned over the years, as I have watched best men who are past friends of the bride, that the groom becomes rather jealous when he sees other men flirting with his bride-to-be. Her love belongs to him, not to others. Christ is not any different. When I see pastors, leaders, and other shepherds flirting with the church to get them to fall in love with them, I shudder to think of the day when the Groom returns for his bride. We had better remember who the bride and the Groom are! The good news is that a splinter of the future has invaded our time in the Person and work of Jesus Christ. We can take an advanced loan, right now, on the riches of our future lives together. What a way to serve Christ! What a day to serve Christ!

Summary

1. We live in several family systems at the same time. Like a frog, we can live in two different worlds, simultaneously. These **relational networks** (our families of origin, the ones we marry into, and our church families) **impact each other**. We cannot be so naïve as to think someone's response is confined to the relational world we are in. Having an extended family means that there are currents we do not see pushing on the boats of those with whom we desire to relate.

2. Problems in one relational system can surface in another system. An enmeshed home system will affect how a worker relates to his co-workers. The good news is that the reverse is also true. **Healing one network can create positive results in another network**. Teaching the cross-racial relationships that are needed to be healthy, by staying differentiated, can in turn free up other churches we do not see.

3. Both black and white churches do a lot of **in-house preaching**. When we find ourselves in anxious, confrontational situations, we must be careful not to over own or to personalize. Sorry, but we may not be that important to the other church! The black or the white church may just be trying to stabilize a stressful relationship inside by triangling in a common, safe issue. Do not take the bait.

CONCLUSION
Connecting the Dots

It was an auction of a wealthy estate. The deceased was a bit eccentric. He had lost his only son in the Korean War. His wife had died some time ago. His furniture and personal items were auctioned off first. Though bored with the bidding on these items, the crowd remained because they knew the elderly gentleman had one of the greatest art and sculpture collections in the region. Finally, the last personal item was held high. It was a simple, framed picture of the old man's son. The picture was a bit faded. The son was in his military uniform.

"What is the bid for this item?" the auctioneer asked. There was silence. He asked again. "Will anyone bid anything for this?"

From the back of the crowd, a well-dressed, middle-aged man yelled, "Someone bid something, so we can get on with that precious art collection. That's why we all came!"

The people chuckled and agreed, "Yes!"

At last, an older, modestly dressed woman ventured, "I'll bid twenty-five dollars. I was the maid here long ago, and I know what that picture meant to the mister. That's my bid. That's what I have."

"Sold!" the auctioneer cried, "for twenty-five dollars." Then, he ended the gathering. "Thank you, ladies and gentlemen, for coming today. I do hope you enjoy your purchases."

"What?!" they cried. "You must be joking. What about auctioning the art?"

"Oh," the estate auctioneer explained, "the estate will and trust were very clear. The deceased bequeathed all his art, sculptures, and paintings to the man or the woman who cared enough about the memory of his son to purchase his picture."

He then turned to the elderly woman with a smile, "Madam, do enjoy your fortune."

A Journey for Fortune and Glory

Similarly, there is a fortune waiting for those who know what is on our Heavenly Father's heart. He promises the wealth of the King of Kings to all those who cherish his Son. The Apostle Paul wrote, "we are heirs – heirs of God, and co heirs with Christ, if indeed we share in his sufferings in order that we may also share in his glory" (Romans 8:17). We are filthy rich, and we do not know it.

Jesus never said that the desire to be fulfilled was wrong. In fact, he said this is so legitimate that trying to fulfill this desire with what the world offers is foolish. Christ never said, "Don't be rich." He said that we can be rich in heaven, where it really pays and where our riches are always safe (Matthew 6:19, 20). Christ never said, "Don't seek approval and glory." He said that we are not to seek the passing approval of the crowd or the temporary high of personal achievements. Instead, we are to seek the glory and the applause that he gives. (Consider Matthew 6:1-4.)

There are treasures in the family of God. They are treasures hidden just below the surface of the strained relationships we so lightly snub and ignore. I have found these treasures! As with all expeditions into uncharted lands, finding these jewels comes at a price of hurt, tears, and struggle. But, man, oh, man, what a pay off! You can actually use the currents of family systems to steer your boat of dreams ahead and to reach the final destination.

Let me ask you several questions. How far would you travel to discover a lost city of gold, emeralds, and diamonds? How much effort would you put forth to unlock the secret of a vaccination that would keep your loved ones from ever having cancer or heart disease? Are you ready to take the first step in loving what Christ loves – his bride, the church?

It Is Not How You Play the Game, but Where You Play It

Although I have learned a wealth of lessons in my journey thus far, let me summarize the most crucial one: Family systems is simply understanding that people do what they do more on the basis of how they relate in any given relational network than on the basis of their personality traits. Therefore, in understanding the dynamics of the urban and the suburban church, I have applied the five basic principles of relationships.

The first principle of relational systems is **homeostasis**. No one likes change. Once a system is established, it will resist any change that threatens to disrupt its equilibrium, even if the change is for the better. These behaviors are not conscious. This is just how systems work.

The second dynamic of systems is the **identified patient**. This means that the neediest person (group, organization) or the person (group, organization) with the most symptoms may not be the sickest one. Very often, people are positioned into being the dent in the pavement into which all the toxins run. Some unfunctioning people are not so unbalanced. They may simply be in the position to absorb the illness of the system. It is like a gas trap under a sink. This pipe is not any different from any other pipe. The gas pipe is simply positioned and curved to trap the noxious gas from the sewer underneath. Sometimes, our sick communities are simply manifesting the illness of other apparently healthy communities. We are connected.

The third principle is **differentiation**, the power of presence. The answer and the tremendous advantage of this unconscious dynamic are that we can bring about healing without anyone knowing it. The answer is to stay in touch and to define what we are about.

The fourth principle of relationships is **triangling**. When two people or two groups are uncomfortable with each other, they pull a third person, group, or issue into the system to divert the anxiety. What Peter tells you about Paul has to do with you and Peter's relationship; it is not about Paul.

The fifth and final principle focuses on **the extended family**. Unseen players are on the field. We all live in several relational systems at any given time. A problem in one network can manifest itself in another. Likewise, healing one network by staying in touch and defining can actually bring positive results inside a different network.

Where to Begin

Every journey must have a starting point. First, I highly recommend reading Dr. Friedman's book, *Generation to Generation*. It is the best work on the study of family systems and church congregations that I have found. Then, here are a few items to keep in mind when making the journey into the reconciliation of relationships.

- **Implement large and small gatherings**

Deciding which is better all depends on the objective. My wife's brother is a squadron commander for F-16s in the United States Air Force. The first executive director at my church worked at the Pentagon and taught at the Army's War College. Though serving for different branches of the military, these two leaders agreed on one point: You must rule the skies if you want to win on land. But, at the same time, you can own the air and not occupy a single foot of ground.

I see the large, highly visible events such as Promise Keeper rallies, Billy Graham crusades, and Campus Crusade for Christ's city-wide fasting gatherings as the air war. Each is a high-profile, high-energy movement in a given city. We found gatherings, such as the National Day of Prayer and Denver LINK, to be tremendous tools in teaching the media and our fellow churches that we really are one in Christ.

But, to occupy a city spiritually, as with a military campaign, we have to grind it out one house at a time. The common foot soldier cannot be replaced. Our military learned in World War II, Vietnam, Desert Storm, and even the Baltic, that if we wanted to occupy, we had to put grunts in the mud. The same is true in our churches. A few families in a few churches of different colors and heritages must share a meal or must spend time together in worship and in prayer in order for us to journey together.

- **Remember, we cannot help a relationship we are not in, and we cannot help a relationship we are stuck in.**

The best place on earth to begin a relationship with another person is on our knees. Prayer is the most effective tool I have seen for cutting through most of the games, smoke, and mirrors we encounter in cross-racial work. Prayer is between you and the Lord, not between you and the person next to you. The side splash of honesty and cleansing that comes from being in the Father's presence is unparalleled. Keep in mind that the dynamics of family systems will work for or against us depending on the Holy Spirit's filling in the new relationship.

Initiate prayer concerts with churches in your area. The Concerts of Prayer, the Lighthouse Movement, and the Pastor's Prayer Summits are a few of the grand, new movements of God in our land. Organize large, city-wide gatherings; or invite different sections of the city to gather for worship, music, and general networking.

The ability to profile and to see all of the great ways in which God is working in the city is eye opening. I highly recommend reading Jack Dennison's book, *City Reaching*, for a fresh and comprehensive study of community transformation.

- **The journey requires that we step onto the other group's turf.**

This is not about playing it safe. This is about stepping onto the turf of others so that we take the initiative to reduce their level of anxiety. Extended family issues will press in, but being on their turf communicates that what is important to them is important to us.

Buckets of ministry gatherings, clergy luncheons, and issue clustering can be found in your city. If you are black, go to the white gatherings first. Then, invite them into your arena. If you are white, go to the African-American gatherings and love, listen, and enjoy. Shake up the system in a positive way by swapping across racial lines preachers and choirs for a Sunday service. This provides a wealth of relational and spiritual fruit for the buck.

Colorado Community Church has turned our fortress into a relational base camp. We have by design half of our people (and their money) involved at the base camp and the other half in other churches and ministries. Of our six pastors, half are African-American and half are Anglo. Even though one of our campuses is mostly Anglo, the presence, the love, and the leadership of the African-American pastors helps to broaden the culture of that congregation. We have also experimented with paying the salaries of pastors of color in the city and then benefiting from their ministry to us on a part-time basis. The goal is the same as we teach and build relationships outside of our comfort zones.

A Word about Politics

Do not be afraid of politics. Do not be infatuated with politics either. Jesus said that we would be able to drink poison and handle serpents and not be harmed (Mark 16:18). Dealing with political issues is living proof. I have found that there is no way to talk about changing a city for Christ without having political issues climb inside the boat. Why? Politics is nothing more than group relationships. Painting with a very broad brush, I will tell you what I have seen.

Because we live in a fallen world, where sin has infected every area, and because we live in a nation governed by a free democracy, we will always disagree in the church about the prioritization of the values of the Kingdom. We want justice, holiness, freedom, and love. We place importance on helping our fellow human, punishing the wicked, upholding sexual purity, raising our own children, and caring for the elderly. Because there is no pure party that embraces these values from a biblical vantage point, both Democrats and Republicans have devout Christians of profound convictions. They also have some sin-infected, worldly, self-absorbed cheese balls! The church's response throughout the ages has been to

- withdraw from society and live in our Christian caves,
- withdraw from society by creating a sub-culture of Christians,
- go along with society and endure until Christ returns, or
- be salt and light to try to transform culture.

Obviously, I vote for the last one. We pick the political boat that we believe will best carry on the forefront of the party platform those issues that we hold the dearest. This means that in our free democracy for the sake of one value we will reluctantly let another issue slide. (We need to remember not to become triangled into these issues relationally. We should have deep convictions based upon the Word of God, but we must not take the bait of sabotage and seduction. We have entered into the region of adult-level homeostasis when we say politics.)

White suburban churches, on the whole, embrace the Republican party for the sake of moral issues. Issues such as abortion, homosexuality, pornography, and abstinence are on the "A" list. Why? The matters surrounding economics, education, and health are rather stable. Black urban churches, on the whole, embrace the Democratic party and the matters of education, job training, health, the elderly, and the judicial system (police, prisons, and courts). Why? These are the hurts and the frustrations in their day-to-day lives. If we could combine the two areas, we would have the kingdom.

The way we each view government also makes a difference. From King David's lean government to his son Solomon's larger government, various viewpoints have been debated. Imagine that government is viewed as an octopus. Numerous tentacles reach into our lives. If we think that the octopus is a mean, self-serving creature (but one that we must have to some degree), we will keep its tentacles short and pruned so that it will not grab us and use us for itself. This is the Republican perspective. On the other hand, if we believe that the octopus is basically a good and friendly creature, whose tentacles reach out to help and who desires to share the bounty of the sea with everyone, then we want these tentacles to grow. This is the classic Democratic view.

Why do I bring this up when writing about uniting the body of Christ? It is for the sheer reason of helping to depower some of the fiercest triangling storms that will rock our boats. Remember, we need to keep in touch and to define!

You Do unto Self as You Do unto Others

If the Lord grants me another ten years of life on this planet, I cannot wait to see the truths in this book played out. I believe it will be all the more reinforced as to how powerful and liberating these truths are. I really do pray that everyone will find what I have discovered: the personal freedom in their own family systems and the dazzling riches of God's people in other skin packages.

My desire is to be the opposite of the grumbling construction worker who felt that the wealthy owner he worked for had cut him out of his fair share. The owner was having a new house built on the hill. To get even, because he knew the old codger did not know a hoot about construction, the worker cut corners by buying shoddy building materials. He left studs out of the walls. He used the cheapest plumbing by tearing out used plumbing from other houses. He did not grade the land right, and he built the new house over a drainage problem. He was determined to get his final payment and take off. He could care less if the building fell apart in two years. He was out of there!

When the house was finished, the owner approached the worker and said, "I know that you have worked for me all these years. I know that at times my cash flow could not pay you much. But, I know this surprise will make it all worth it. Rather than paying you cash, here are the keys. The house you built is your reward!"

Our Lord said, "Whoever finds his life will lose it, and whoever loses his life for my sake will find it (Matthew 10:39). I pray each of us will let the control of our family relationships free in the church and the city so that we can have them back, renewed, and transformed. Give 'em heaven!

SELECTED READINGS

Anderson, James. *The Management of Ministry: Leadership, Purpose, Structure and Community*. New York: Harper and Row, 1988.

Anderson, Ray and Dennis Gurnsey. *On Being Family: A Social Theology of the Family*. Grand Rapids, MI: William Eerdsmans Publishing Company, 1985.

Anderson, Ray. *Minding God's Business*. Grand Rapids, MI: William B. Eerdsmans Publishing Company, 1986.

Blaswick, Jack O. and Judith K. Balswick. *The Family: A Christian Perspective on the Contemporary Home*. Grand Rapids, MI: Baker Book Company, 1989.

Below, Patrick J., George L. Morrisey and Betty Acomb. *The Executive Guide to Strategic Planning*. San Francisco: Jossey-Baass, 1987.

Brown, Colin, ed. *The New International Dictionary of New Testament Theology, Vol. 2, G-Pre*. Grand Rapids, MI: Regency Reference Library, 1976.

Bryan, Barry W. *Strategic Planning Workbook for Nonprofit Organizations*. Management Support Systems, Amherst Wilder Foundation, 1985.

Campbell, Thomas and Gary Reirson. *The Gift of Administration:*

A Theological Basis for Ministry. Philadelphia: Westminster Press, 1981.

Drucker, Peter. *Innovation and Entreprenuership*. New York: Harper and Row, 1985.

______________. *Managing in Turbulent Times*. New York: Harper and Row, 1980.

DuPree, Max. *Leadership is an Art*. New York: Bantam Doubleday Dell Publishing, 1989.

Friedman, Edwin. *Generation to Generation*. New York: Guildford Press, 1985.

Kotler, Philip and Alan Andreasen. *Strategic Marketing for Non-Profit Organizations*. Englewood Cliffs, NJ: Prentice-Hall, 1981.

Ladd, George Eldon. *A Theology of the New Testament*. Grand Rapids, MI: Williams Eerdmans Publishing Company, 1974.

Leas, Speed and Paul Kittlaus. *Church Fights: Managing Conflict in the Local Church*. Philadelphia: The Westminster Press, 1977.

Lewis, C.S. *Miracles*. New York: Macmillan Publishing Company, Inc. 1947.

McGee, Robert and Jim Craddock. *Your Parents and You: How our Parents Shape our Self Concept, our Perception of God, and our Relationships with Others*. Houston, TX: Rapha Publishing, 1990.

McGinnis, Alan. *The Friendship Factor: How to Get Closer to the People You Care for*. Minneapolis: Augsburg Publishing, 1979.

Morrisey, George L., Betty Acomb and Patrick J. Below. *The Executive Guide to Operational Planning*. San Francisco: Jossey-Bass, 1988.

Niebuhr, H. Richard. *Christ and Culture*. New York: Harper & Row, Publishers, 1951.

Peters, Thomas. *Thriving on Chaos: Handbook for Management Revolution*. New York: Harper & Row, 1988.

Sandford, John and Paul Sandford. *Restoring the Christian Family* Tulsa, OK: Victory House, Inc., 1979.

Schaller, Lyle. *Effective Church Planning*. Nashville: Abingdon Press, 1979.

Schein, Edgar H. *Organizational Culture and Leadership*. San Francisco: Jossey-Bass, 1987.

Springle, Pat. *Codependency: A Christian Perspective on Breaking Free from the Hurts and Manipulation of Dysfunctional Relationships*. Houston TX: Rapha Publishing, 1990.

Steiner, George. *Strategic Planning: What Every Manager Must Know*. New York: Free Press, 1979.

Visher, Emily and John Visher. *Stepfamilies: A Guide to Working with Stepparents and Stepchildren*. New York: Brunner/Mazel Publishing, 1979.

Washington, Raleigh and Glen Kehrien. *Breaking Down Walls*. Chicago: Moody Press, 1993.

Wilson, Charles R. *Sojourners in a Land of Promise: Planning, Theology, and Surprise*. Spiritual Growth Resources, Organizational Resources Press, 1981.

Zenger, John, Ed Musselwhite, Kathleen Hurson, and Craig Perrin. *Leading Teams: Mastering the New Roles*. Homewood, IL: Business One Irwin, 1994.

ABOUT THE AUTHOR

Gifted by God as a visionary, leader, and teacher, Dr. Mark Brewer is the senior pastor of Colorado Community Church in the Denver suburb of Englewood. His passion for the reconciliation of the urban and the suburban church communities is evident in the mission statement of this church, the strong relationships he has established with inner-city pastors, and the leadership he has provided for a number of city-wide gatherings. Prior to accepting this position, he served as pastor for churches in Detroit, Michigan; Englewood, Colorado; and Los Angeles, California.

Dr. Brewer also hosts a national radio program, "A New Day for America." His numerous interviews with business professionals, community activists, church and government leaders, health experts, teachers, and authors have contributed significantly to the insights shared in this book.

Brewer completed his undergraduate work at Colorado State University and earned his master's and doctorate from Fuller Seminary. He completed further doctoral work at St Andrew's in Scotland. He and his wife, Carolyn, live in Castle Rock, Colorado. They have three children: Vanessa, Paul, and Rachel.

FOR MORE INFORMATION

Obtain additional copies of this book and information regarding speeches, radio programs, seminars, audio or videotapes by writing or calling

Dr. Mark Brewer
Colorado Community Church/ A New Day for America
3651 South Colorado Boulevard
Englewood, Colorado 80110
303-783-3838